Catholic Inner-City Schools: The Future

By

Dr. Thomas Vitullo-Martin

U.S. Catholic Conference Department of Education, 1979

1979
Publications Office
UNITED STATES CATHOLIC CONFERENCE
1312 Massachusetts Avenue, N.W.
Washington, D.C. 20005

TABLE OF CONTENTS

CATHOLIC INNER-CITY SCHOOLS: THE FUTURE

In 1977 the U.S. Catholic Conference Department of Education commissioned the present work to be written in an effort to better define and determine the urgent needs of Catholics in the inner-city. Opening with the question, "Are Catholic inner-city schools closing faster than Catholic schools elsewhere?", the four chapters raise many crucial questions about economic, social, political and demographic problems presently confronting these schools.

Although author Dr. Thomas Vitullo-Martin is quick to point out that more research is needed to understand more fully the problems of inner-city schools, it is evident from the position he takes that these schools can no longer rely on past modes of operation for survival. New philosophies that respond to present-day situations must be constructed. A re-thinking of financial and administrative structures must be undertaken. Dynamic models need to be identified if commitment to these schools is to remain strong.

The work contained herein is one of many positions concerning the real issues that face inner-city schools. It is hoped that these reflections will inspire a new surge of interest and research which will bring a renewed vigor to our schools and the persons they serve.

Special thanks must be given to: Msgr. Wilfrid H. Paradis, Secretary of Education, USCC, Ms. Elly Murphy, Editor, and Ms. Charlett Bundy, Production Manager of the USCC Department of Education. Gratitude is also extended to Bishop Francis J. Stafford, D.D., Dr. Otto Kraushaar, the education departments of the Archdioceses of Philadelphia, New York and Detroit for their suggestions on the substance and flow of the initial draft of the study; the Boys Town Research Center for Youth Development at Catholic University, and Ms. Phyllis L. Brantley who typed the manuscript.

Eugene F. Hemrick
Director of Research, NCCB/USCC

Introduction

The Bureau of the Census 1975 Survey of Income and Education found that 10% of the 48 million elementary and secondary students attend private schools, and that these schools enrolled a far greater proportion of lower-income students than most people believe. The survey ranked families by their cash income from all sources (ignoring in-kind income, such as the provision of free housing) and determined whether their school-aged children attended public or private schools. The census bureau's survey found that (1) nationwide 6% of the students from the lowest-income families (cash income below $1,000 per year) are enrolled in private schools; and (2) in the North Central and Northeastern states, the figure is 9%. The survey, as reported, does not distinguish between enrollment in elementary and secondary schools. If it did, the precentages of the lowest-income students in private schools would be even higher, because higher tuitions at the high school level prevent as many lower-income students from attending those schools.

Private schools enroll not only substantial portions of the low-income population, but disproportionately high numbers of minority students as well. In more than half the Western states, private schools have higher (percentage) minority enrollments than public. For example, 57% of New Mexico's private schools are minority as opposed to 48% of its public schools, according to a 1970 study by the Department of Health, Education and Welfare's Office of Civil Rights. HEW's National Center for Educational Statistics found that, in the West, the enrollment of black students in private schools more than doubled between 1970 and 1975, and that in private elementary schools there were actually more used by blacks, with 7.4% of all black students enrolled in private schools, and only 6.6% white students enrolled.

Most lower-income and minority students in private schools are enrolled in inner-city schools, and more than 75% of all private inner-city schools are Catholic schools. The United States Catholic Conference commissioned this study to review the literature and other available information describing Catholic inner-city schools, and to aid in reviewing church policies concerning these schools.

Shortly after the study began, an incident in New York City received national news coverage, highlighting the importance of thinking through these policies. In the spring of 1977, Our Lady of Victory School in the South Bronx projected a deficit of $10,000 for the following school year. The low-income parish had been

1

devastated by fire, and parish administrators projected a spiraling increase. Parents and community leaders protested the closing, arguing that it would hurt the children and drive from the neighborhood many of the families who played important roles in resisting the forces destroying the South Bronx. The Congress of Racial Equality (CORE) offered to raise funds to cover the school's deficit, and eventually assumed all control over and liability for the school. The now renamed CORE Community School kept most of our Lady of Victory's staff and students.

Why was CORE willing to cover the school's deficit when the archdiocese was not? The community needed the school, but the archdiocese decided other schools were more important, perhaps schools with more Catholic parishioners to help support them, perhaps some with better chances of survival. Is the archdiocese beginning to practice triage? Or did it take a position it should have taken regardless of available financial resources? Is the Catholic life best served by funding the school, or by other pastoral activities, given limited funds? If these schools are so valuable to their communities, why can't they support themselves? Are they really valuable? How do they help their neighborhoods? Can the (arch)dioceses increase available resources to aid these schools? How much more aid will they need?

This study presents no original research. It simply attempts to look at existing information on inner-city Catholic schools, to summarize what we know, and to state the questions that church policymakers, clergy or lay, must ask.

Thomas Vitullo-Martin

2

CHAPTER 1

INNER-CITY CATHOLIC SCHOOLS FACE SERIOUS PROBLEMS

In the past ten years, many inner-city Catholic schools have closed, apparently as part of a general pattern of Catholic school reduction, caused principally by cultural and demographic changes beyond the church's control. But this is a false picture. The inner-city schools are declining for different reasons and are in a special crisis. As the rest of the Catholic system reaches an equilibrium, the condition of the inner-city schools will continue to deteriorate. For a while in the early 1970s, the church seemed to have arrested their decline. But within the next few years, many of these schools will disappear, for the church appears to have reached its organizational limits for their support.

The problem is filled with ironies. Today's Catholics have more resources to support these schools, but less reason to support them. Enrolling as they do substantial numbers of Protestants, Jews, and other religious and non-religious people, the schools serve public purposes more than traditional Catholic ones. The church appears to have become the most powerful religious body in the country, but has not yet made public purposes its own purposes. Support for inner-city Catholic schools will require a redefinition of what the church regards as its mission, and will require important organizational and political changes in its structure. The church is likely to change, but can it adjust before these schools close?

Table 1

CATHOLIC MEMBERSHIP, BY ETHNICITY AND RACE, 1970-77

Racial or Ethnic Group	Percent of Group Catholic, 1977	Number Catholic 1970	Number Catholic 1977
Black	4.1%	870,000	1,000,000
*Spanish-Surnamed	45.0%	3,500,000	5,000,000
Oriental	—	—	—
American Indian	—	—	—
Other	22.1%	41,000,000	40,200,000
TOTAL	22.0%	45,400,000	46,200,000

* There are 11 million Spanish-surnamed residents of the U.S. (see Table

3

5). Almost all of them share a Catholic culture, but relatively few of them are organizationally affiliated with the U.S. Catholic Church. This complicates our estimates of Catholic population. In 1965, Greeley and Rossi found only 5% of U.S. Catholics were Spanish-surnamed, in their national sample of the U.S. population for identifying the effects of Catholic schooling (see Table 1A Appendix). They further found this group to be the least likely to have attended Catholic elementary and secondary schools exclusively, as Table 7 shows. They found 2,250,000 Spanish-surnamed Catholics. Their figures are likely to differ from parish figures since Spanish who are not organizationally affiliated are nonetheless likely to identify themselves as Catholic. On the other hand, their survey may have substantially undercounted the Spanish-surnamed population because of the difficulties attached to surveying Spanish-surnamed residents as part of any general survey, particularly the fact that an extremely high proportion of Spanish-surnamed Americans speak little or no English. (The Bureau of the Census found in 1975 that 85% of all Spanish-surnamed Americans reported that Spanish is the language usually spoken in the household.)

We are using the Greeley and Rossi estimate as our base for 1965 and further estimating that this number increased substantially in the next 12 years through immigration, and about doubled—hence our estimate of 5 million. Sociologist Joseph Fitzpatrick reports that 25% of all U.S. Catholics are Spanish-surnamed.[6a] His estimate agrees with PADRES and the Northeast Pastoral Center for Hispanics: There are 11 million Hispanic or Spanish-surnamed Catholics in the U.S.[6b] The difference between our estimate and Fitzpatrick's rests solely on the degree of institutional connection we are requiring before we include Spanish-surnamed Catholics in the general Catholic census.

More is at stake than inner-city schools. The future ethnic composition of the American Catholic Church is involved: Will Spanish, French and English-speaking immigrants from Latin-American and Caribbean countries remain or become Catholic?

Since the early 1960s, virtually the entire expansion of the American Catholic population is the result of increases of Spanish-surnamed Catholics, who now comprise about 25% of all American Catholics (See Table 1). However, the Spanish are more culturally than institutionally active Catholics, and only 5%-10% of *active* parishioners are Spanish-surnamed (See Table 1A, Appendix). The American church needs institutions to link Spanish Catholics to the parishes. Although some Spanish immigrants are settling in rural areas, most come to the older, inner areas of large and medium-sized cities where Catholic inner-city schools exist. These schools could be especially important in connecting recent Spanish-surnamed immigrants to the American church, and their closing may prove to be extremely costly. The record for the past decade is not good. There are fewer Spanish-surnamed students in Catholic schools today than there were in 1970. (See Table 2).

Table 2

CHANGE IN CATHOLIC ELEMENTARY SCHOOL
ENROLLMENT, 1970-77, BY ETHNICITY

	Enrolled in Roman Catholic School, 1970		Enrolled in Roman Catholic School, 1977	
	Percent	Number	Percent	Number
Black	5.2	174,000	7.6	184,646
Spanish-Surnamed	6.4	215,000	8.3	199,664
Oriental	1.5	17,000	1.2	28,592
American Indian	1.5	15,000	1.3	6,305
Other	87.4	2,935,000	82.6	1,996,792
TOTAL		3,356,000		2,415,999

Source: NCEA, *U.S. Catholic Schools,* 1970-77; NCES, *Condition of Education,* 1975-77

Catholic inner-city schools are binding the church more closely to the black community. Today, only 1.5% of all Catholics are black, but 11.5% of all Americans are black. Only about 4% of American blacks are Catholic. Because of inner-city schools, the Catholic church is more important to blacks than these membership figures suggest. Almost 8% of all Catholic elementary school children are black, and approximately 40% of these students are not Catholic. (Typically, those black students who are Catholic have one parent who is not Catholic). More than half of all blacks in Catholic schools (and about two-thirds of all minorities) are enrolled in inner-city Catholic schools. The loss of these schools will prove extremely costly to the American church. If they close, the Catholic church will be a white church in an integrated America.

Almost half of all inner-city school students are not counted as minorities but many of these are recent immigrants (for example, Greeks, Italians and Lebanese) to whom the American Church has a particular responsibility. In general, Catholic inner-city schools are disproportionately important to the church's commitment to the poor, minorities, and the powerless. From the viewpoint of inner-city residents, the schools are important beyond their numbers. They typically work more closely with inner-city families than do public schools, are academically superior, and provide a moral and religious training many parents believe is not available in inner-city public schools.

In the remainder of this chapter, I will argue that the inner-city schools have been in a crisis, one that has been masked for a number of reasons, and that the church has already aided these schools far more than it has acknowledged and at a level far beyond its resources—setting the scene for a dramatic collapse. Because of the size of its efforts, which have been much less successful than it has thought, the church has fewer options available to deal with the basic problems. This chapter will begin to inventory some of the approaches used to aid the schools, but the church needs a more systematic inventory and description of what has been attempted, and with what effect in each diocese.

This study will focus on elementary schools. First, because the problems of inner-city Catholic education begin at the parish or elementary school level and must be solved there. Second, solving the problems of inner-city elementary schools would solve most of the problems of the secondary schools. Third, concentrating on the elementary schools allows us to discuss the central problems more simply.

Inner-City School Closings—a Hidden Crisis

For some time, available statistics seemed to indicate that Catholic inner-city schools were doing well—especially compared to other Catholic schools. Church officials believed that the steps they had initiated in the late 1960s to help these schools were effective. They were mistaken, in part because of a statistical problem stemming from the fact that the category "inner-city" included more territory in each succeeding census year, and in part because they did not realize the full extent of the aid they had been giving the schools, and therefore could not fully assess the size of the problem they would face when the funds ran out.

In the early 1970s it seemed as if the church had solved the problem of inner-city school closings, which the National Catholic Education Association (NCEA) had first identified in its Catholic school censuses of the 1967-70 period. By 1970, 16% of all Catholic inner-city schools had closed, in a period in which only 1% of Catholic urban (but not inner-city) schools disappeared. Dioceses then made extraordinary efforts to subsidize inner-city schools, and their efforts appeared successful. Between 1970-73, NCEA reported that only 4% of the inner-city schools had closed, some of which were consolidations. Catholic inner-city schools lost only 2% of their population in the period and appeared to be the healthiest of all Catholic schools by location. Catholic urban, suburban, small town and rural schools lost 19% to 24% of their enrollments.

6

However, the record looked better than it actually was. NCEA cautioned that some schools had shifted from urban to inner-city between census years, and that this should affect interpretation of trends. The data problem was that inner-city areas had grown rapidly in the late 1960s and early 1970s, and many schools identifying themselves as urban on the 1967 census changed their designation to inner-city in later censuses. Thus, if no schools closed, the inner-city schools would have increased in number substantially. We do not know how many schools made this switch, nor when they made it. We know from diocesan sources that many schools closed during the period, but we do not know how many of those were in the inner-city. On the NCEA census sheets, schools identified themselves as urban or inner-city, and NCEA believed that a school's self-reclassification from urban to inner-city accounts for "part of the large decrease in urban and the small decrease in inner-city enrollments." Such shifts obscured the alarming rate at which inner-city schools were closing.

On Table 3 we find the original NCEA count of the number of Catholic schools urban and inner-city for the 1967-73 period. We can see that the decline of schools in the inner-city was by no means insignificant for the period. They declined 20% compared to 10% for urban schools. Inner-city schools appear to have closed at twice the rate of urban schools, even before we have accounted for switches between the urban and inner-city categories.

Table 3 shows an incredible trend, which forces us to take account of the switches. The urban category shows an alarming increase in closings in the pre-1970 and post-1970 periods, from 1% in 1967-70 to 10% in 1970-73. Inner-city schools, on the other hand, show a substantially improved rate of closings, from 16% in the pre-1970 period, to 4% post-1970. If these statistics were correct, this meant the church was permitting large numbers of urban schools to close in the post-1970 period, while making strenuous efforts to save inner-city schools. The inner-city schools, as we shall see, are disproportionately non-Catholic and the church would have preserved non-catholic schools at the expense of schools heavily Catholic. The position is unlikely, and certainly unreported.

It is more likely that "switching" affected the statistics, and we have taken a reasonable guess about how much has taken place. Let us assume that at least half the urban schools NCEA counted as closing in the 1970-73 period simply became inner-city schools. Then urban schools would have lost only 5% by their numbers to closings in the second period, a reasonable increase over the 1% of the first period. But inner-city schools would have lost 16%, the same rate of decline as in the first period. If our assumption is approximately correct, at least 30% of the schools identified as inner-city in 1967 closed by 1973. *Inner-city schools actually closed at almost five times the rate of urban schools.*

Table 3

DECLINE IN NUMBERS OF URBAN AND INNER-CITY CATHOLIC ELEMENTARY SCHOOLS, UNADJUSTED AND ADJUSTED FOR RECLASSIFICATION OF ERROR, 1967-73

	Number of Schools			
	Unadjusted			Adjusted*
School Location	1967	1970	1973	1973
Urban	3,123	3,092	2,797	2,945
Inner City	1,490	1,246	1,200	1,052

	Percent Change				
	Unadjusted			Adjusted*	
School Location	1967-1970	1970-1973	1967-1973	1970-1973	1967-1973
Urban	−1%	−10%	−10%	−5%	−6%
Inner City	−16%	−4%	−20%	−16%	−29%

Note: Categories "urban" and "inner-city" are self-ascribed on NCEA census sheets completed by each Catholic school.

* Adjusted by attributing 50% of the loss of schools in the urban category between 1970 and 1973 to self-ascribed reclassification of the school as inner-city. (Hence 147 *fewer* urban schools actually closed and 147 *more* inner-city schools closed than unadjusted statistics indicate.)

Source: NCEA, U.S. Catholic Schools, 1973-74, p. 7 Table 2 (recalculated).

The Decline Continues

NCEA's most recent Catholic school census suggests a continuous decline of inner-city schools. Its 1977-78 census does not identify Catholic schools by location, but we can still get an idea of how inner-city schools have fared by examining the enrollment patterns of black elementary school students. Black enrollment is a good indicator of the condition of inner-city schools (even though whites outnumber blacks by more than two to one in these schools) because 54% of all blacks in Catholic schools are in inner-city schools (1970). It is highly likely, given the racial composition of the inner-cities with the largest number of Catholic schools, that a decline in black enrollments means inner-city schools have closed.

We immediately run into a problem analogous to the one caused by switching the school categories. The white Catholic school population dropped dramatically—32%—from 1970 to 1977. The loss of so many white students naturally meant that the blacks would increase their percentage presence in Catholic schools even if they did not increase in actual numbers. This is exactly what has happened. Blacks increased their presence from 5.2% to 7.8% of all Catholic students since 1970. Numerically, black enrollments peaked about 1972. By the next racial census, 1977, blacks *lost* 16,350 students, a decline of almost 10%. In the 1970-77 period, Spanish-surnamed student enrollments declined by 7%. The decline in minority enrollments suggests that inner-city schools are in trouble.

Causes of the Decline of White Enrollments Do Not Apply to Minorities

In the 1970-77 period, minority enrollments in Catholic elementary schools remained approximately constant, but should have grown substantially, because the supply of minority students grew. It is true that some contraction of the Catholic system was inevitable because the baby-boom bulge that affected elementary schools in the early 1960s passed, and birth rates dropped below previous levels. But the minority school-aged population continued to grow throughout the period, and young minority families moved into neighborhoods left behind by the maturing white families in the center cities. Minorities should have replaced whites in Catholic schools in much larger numbers, if the schools had been able to serve them as well as they had served the white students. There are, of course, many good reasons why the school *could not* serve the minorities as well, not the least of which is that the incoming groups often differed from the previous residents of a typical changing neighborhood in their language, traditions, and religious affiliation. These reasons are quite different from the ones that explain the decline of white student enrollments, as we shall see. In essence, the white student enrollments declined because there were fewer students; minority enrollments declined because the schools could not, or did not, adapt to changing neighborhoods. Let us examine the declines of the white and minority student enrollments in greater detail.

Decline of white enrollment:

(1) Since 1970, the total U.S. elementary school-aged population has declined by about 12%, (See Table 4). Until recently, Catholics had a higher average family size than the rest of the white population. The maternal decline in birth rate is disproportionately attributable to a decline in Catholic births, principally among white Catholics. White school-aged Catholic population dropped 14% to 16%, which explains more than half the fall-off in Catholic school enrollments of white students.

(2) White Catholics have migrated from cities, where there are many Catholic schools, to suburbs, where the church has not, in the past decade, built new schools to accommodate them.

(3) Similarly, white Catholics have moved from the Northeast and North Central states, where 75% of all Catholic schools are located, to the South and West, which have only 25% of the schools. In the 1970-75 period alone, the Northeast lost 3%, and the North Central states 2%, of their school-aged populations to the South and West, which gained 3% and 2% respectively through immigration. No new Catholic schools were built in the receiving regions to serve the incoming Catholic students.

(4) A substantial proportion of the white Catholic population has less need for Catholic schools today, not because the schools have changed, or because the church is less relevant to the families, but because their social status and their relationship to the public schools has changed. Irish and Italians, the two largest Catholic ethnic groups, have now the highest median incomes of all American ethnic groups after Jews. This has two important consequences for Catholic schools.

First, wealthier Catholics from the city tend to cluster in the suburbs. Suburban governments find they have a high percentage of Catholics in their population. In the normal course of events, Catholics will gain political control of their public school system. In such cases, the school board, the school staff, and most of the students will be Catholic. Hence, there will be no clear religious or cultural differences between the public schools and the Catholic schools, not because the Catholic schools are so secular but because the public schools are so Catholic. What obvious reasons are there for supporting separate Catholic schools in these communities? The same student would be taught by virtually the same teachers in public or Catholic schools.

Second, public schools have the edge in these communities because they are much better funded and the tax system makes them much cheaper to support. The neighborhood public schools serving upper-income families are generally lavishly funded in comparison to the Catholic schools in those communities. For example, in one of the wealthiest communities in the New York metropolitan area, the public schools spent $8,426 per pupil in 1977. The Catholic school in this area spent about $1,200

Table 4

ELEMENTARY SCHOOL-AGED POPULATION (6-13), 1972 TO 1978, BY ETHNICITY

Racial Group	Total Population 1975	Population, Aged 6 to 13, for Entire Group			Proportion Aged 6-13 1978
		1972*	1975	1977*	
Black	23,400,000	4,177,000	4,135,000	4,091,000	16.9%
Spanish	11,000,000	2,190,000	2,220,000	2,230,000	20.1%
Oriental	2,030,000	255,000	260,000	270,000	12.8%
American Indian	763,594**	162,000	165,000	167,000	21.0%
Other	185,240,000	24,675,000	23,150,000	22,140,000	12.5%
TOTAL	213,137,000	31,880,000	29,880,000	28,595,000	14.0%

* Time-series data for school-aged population for years 1970, 1975, 1980 is presented on Table 1.01, NCES, 1977. The data uses only two racial categories—white and "black and other races." A population breakdown by age and race for 1975 is presented in Table 1.03, NCES, 1977. This breakdown does identify Spanish and isolates black (counting black Spanish as Spanish), but does not identify American Indian. The sample base appears to differ slightly from the base used to estimate total racial population given in the first column. Using the 1975 ethnic data, we have extrapolated time-series data for ethnic school-aged population on the total and white time-series data of Table 1.01. Discrepancies as great as 1% exist between the various samples, and the figures given in this table should therefore be understood to be approximately, but not precisely, accurate.

** Data is from 1970.

per pupil, including contributed services. These massive differences in funding are reflected in student achievements. Researchers have found that Catholic students from higher-income families who attend public elementary school tend to outperform similar students attending Catholic schools. The research is certainly not conclusive, and in specific neighborhoods the reverse may be true (for example, a Catholic school in Hollywood Hills has a reputation for excellence which has permitted it to attract a substantial number of Jewish students from the public schools), but it does fit what we generally expect to find.

The competition between public and Catholic schools for upper-income families is made more difficult for the Catholic by

11

the tax system. (This argument is discussed more fully in Chapter 4.) Catholic schools increasingly rely on tuition for income, and tuition (unlike church contributions which formerly supported the schools) are not tax deductible expenses on federal and state income tax returns. Wealthy families, typically pay 40%-70% of their gross income to federal, state and local income taxes. Consequently, they must earn more than twice as much as the nominal cost of the tuition. To pay a tuition of $1,000, the wealthy family must earn $3,333 at the 70% bracket. Put another way, for every $10 increase in tuition to these families, the federal and state governments take an additional $23.30.

In sum, some of the white decline reflects population changes beyond the reach of Catholic schools; some results from the church's failure to build schools for relocating, Catholic families; and some results from changes in the social status or political power of Catholic groups. Public schools reflect the dominant values of a community. As Catholics begin to dominate the community, they find public schools more hospitable and therefore more acceptable. Consequently, they find Catholic schools less necessary.

Decline of Minority Student Enrollment

None of the reasons behind the decline in white enrollments explain the decline in minority Catholic enrollments. The principal reason for white enrollment decline was a lowered birth rate. Blacks too had a lower birth rate which would have lowered the number of school-aged children during the 1970-77 period, but it was very slight in comparison to the white rates, and could not fully explain the drop in black students (Table 4). In fact, the birth rate is simply a measure of potential students and during the 1970-1977 period, the black *Catholic* population increased by about 8,000 per year, so the number of available black students increased despite a slight drop in birth rates for the group. All other minority groups increased their numbers of school-aged students during this period.

Another reason white enrollment declined was that whites moved to areas where there were no Catholic schools. Neither blacks nor Spanish encountered this problem. Both groups expanded the neighborhood-areas they dominated during the 1970s, and in most cases, moved into neighborhoods vacated by Catholic ethnic groups. These neighborhoods already had Catholic schools. More blacks and Spanish live in neighborhoods where there are, or recently were, Catholic schools, but fewer are attending them.

12

White enrollment dropped in part because whites had less need of Catholic schools, since they had great influence in the public schools and had high quality schools available to them. Blacks, in particular, continued to express an unabated demand for Catholic schools. Surveys show that blacks have the highest regard for the academic quality of Catholic schools, and commonly regard them as superior to public schools in inner-city areas. Black parents on an average pay substantially higher Catholic elementary school tuitions than white parents, which is evidence of their continued strong support for the schools. As a rule of thumb, tuitions in schools with high percentages of black students average twice those charged at predominantly white schools in the same diocese.

Even the tax system is less a factor in discouraging Catholic school attendance for the minorities. Income tax rates paid by minority families, since they are a function of family income, are

Chart 1

PERCENTAGE OF CATHOLIC, SCHOOL-AGED STUDENTS (6-13) ENROLLED IN CATHOLIC SCHOOLS, BY ETHNICITY, 1970-77

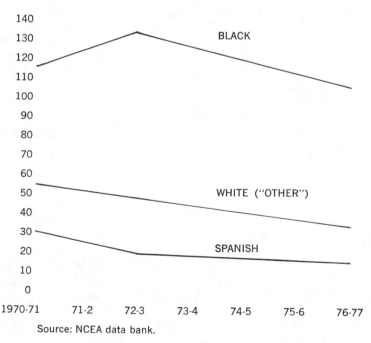

Source: NCEA data bank.

13

lower for minority families, and typically amount to only a 5% to 10% surcharge on the tuition bill (e.g., a family must earn $111 at the 10% tax bracket in order to pay a $100 tuition.)

It is useful to look at changes in the proportions of the school-aged children for each ethnic group attending Catholic schools during the period, as an indication of how well the schools are doing. Chart 1 presents the percentages of school-aged Catholic children enrolled in Catholic schools for each ethnic group from 1970 to 1977. In effect, the chart presents a record of how well the schools did, once we eliminate the distraction caused by increases or declines in the birth rate.* The chart shows that the white decline is not nearly so great as the unadjusted figures suggest. Half of the 30% white decline in Catholic enrollments in the period is accounted for by a 15% decline in white school-aged population. But the adjustment reverses the case for minority students: their school aged population increased during the period, and the increase was greater than the increase in their enrollment in the Catholic schools. Catholic schools are enrolling 9% and 11% fewer blacks and Spanish-surnamed students respectively, after we have adjusted the percentage of enrollments for increases in those groups' school-aged population.

Simply stated, Catholic schools are losing ground in minority enrollments. Only a small proportion of the white student population decline can be attributed to the church's failure to provide or maintain schools, but for minorities, the closing of inner-city schools is the most likely cause of the minority enrollment decline.

Table 5

CHANGE IN ENROLLMENT OF BLACK ELEMENTARY SCHOOL STUDENTS IN PRIVATE SCHOOLS, 1970-75, BY REGION

Region	Enrollment			% Change	
	1970	1972	1975	1970-75	1972-75
Northeast	72,000	97,000	40,000	−44%	−59%
Southeast	45,000	32,000	34,000	−24%	+6%
Central	55,000	37,000	40,000	−27%	+8%
West	25,000	20,000	49,000	+96%	+145%

Source: NCES, *Condition of Education*, 1977, p. 192, Table 4.05.

---

* Chart 1 can be compared to Chart 1A in the Appendix, which presents changes in the percentage of ethnic enrollments without adjusting for changes in student-aged population.

Regional Variations

There are regional differences in the fortunes of inner-city and minority Catholic schools. HEW's National Center for Education Statistics (NCES) has published statistics on black and private school enrollments which permit us to examine more subtly NCEA enrollment trends for blacks. This data shows the problem of inner-city school closings, as revealed by black attendance at private schools, to be far more serious in the Northeast and North Central states than in the West (see Table 5).*

More than 90% of all blacks in private schools are in Catholic schools.* So NCES findings should be describing—approximately—the situation in Catholic schools. They show that between 1970 and 1975, black enrollments in Catholic elementary schools *declined 44%* in the Northeast, 24% in the Southeast, and 27% in the Central states. In the West, total black enrollment almost doubled (+96%) in that period. Catholic elementary schools in the West now enroll higher percentages of blacks than do public elementary schools. The West has only 15% of all black students, but has 30% of all black students enrolled in Catholic elementary schools. The Northeast and Central regions, with twice as many Catholic schools as in the West and 45% of all black students, enroll numerically fewer black students in their Catholic schools.

Overall, then, Catholic schools in the West appear to be quite healthy. But closer examination shows problems. In part, the high percentage of minority enrollments there reflects *under-utilization of Western Catholic schools by whites.* Furthermore, the Spanish-surnamed enrollment changes are the most important minority statistics for the Western schools, but the available statistics do not permit a regional breakdown of changes in Spanish enrollments. We know that, nationally, Spanish-surnamed

---

* Nationally, Catholic and Lutheran schools account for over 95% of black inner-city enrollments. Other religions operate a few inner-city schools, and some unaffiliated schools enroll lower-income inner-city residents. Over 75% of all inner-city schools enrolling lower-income blacks are Catholic, another 6% are Lutheran, 6% independent, and 3% each are Seventh Day Adventist, Baptist, Episcopalian, and other.

The best available data on minority private school enrollments comes from the organizations of private schools. Few states with high percentages of minority students acquire or tabulate any racial statistics for private school enrollments, and federal statistics are either based on state statistics or are projections of one-in-four or one-in-five household surveys or of the current population survey sample. All these data sources tend to understate black private school enrollment even more than they understate total private school enrollment.

student enrollments in Catholic schools dropped 7% between 1970 and 1977 in absolute numbers. Adjusted for population changes, the decline has been almost 11% for that same period (See Chart 1). American Indian enrollments also have declined dramatically, down 60% since 1970. Almost all the declines in both these groups have occurred in the West. In fact, the Western decline for the Spanish-surnamed students has been greater than these statistics indicate, because of the recent great expansion of the Spanish-surnamed Catholic school population in the East. About half of all New York Catholic students are now Spanish-speaking, and large increases have also occurred in the Brooklyn and Miami Catholic systems in the 1970-77 period. The decline in Catholic enrollments of Spanish-surnamed students has come *despite* these new influxes in the East, and has therefore been substantial in the West. We must strain the data to arrive at these conclusions, but they are prudent judgments based on the best data available.

What Have the Dioceses Done?

Although some dioceses are making great efforts to preserve the schools, greater than they know and greater than they can sustain, many inner-city schools are closing or losing ground in enrolling minorities. Because the dioceses have done as much as they have, more inner-city schools have survived than we could reasonably have expected, but the church has virtually exhausted its available resources and has not been able to tap sufficient new sources for funds. To see what the Church can do, we should review what it has done.

It is difficult to analyze the true extent of the fiscal crisis affecting the schools and the dioceses because the Church has traditionally been reluctant to reveal its financing to the public. There are good reasons for this secrecy, but the secrecy has its costs as well. In several dioceses, parish account books are not analyzed by central diocesan officials, or are analyzed only after the parish or school experiences financial difficulties. Information needed for planning and problem-identification is not assembled. Often parishes report to several diocesan officials on different aspects of their financial situation, but this information is not shared in the central offices. This is particularly true in dioceses which have established separate budgets for school and parish. The officials responsible for the schools are often not fully informed of the condition of the parish's finances. To some extent, the need for planning information conflicts with the traditional hierarchical practices of dioceses in which higher diocesan officials receive information about parishes not circulated among lower officials. Also, diocesan planners are often unaware of the financial condition of teaching orders staffing the schools. The combination of secrecy, hierarchy, partial autonomy of parishes and orders, and collectors of information in the central offices increases the difficulty of analysis.

To simplify the review of dioceses on efforts to aid inner-city schools, I have divided the approaches into three categories, according to the sources of the aid money. I will begin with the approaches most fully under the control of the diocese, move to approaches in which the dioceses must rely on contributions from the parishes, and finally examine approaches involving only decisions by non-diocesan authorities—in the parish, religious orders, or the secular community. Whatever the source, some inner-city school aid is acknowledged as aid; other aid is hidden, or simply not accounted as aid. (Note: I have ranked approaches according to the degree of autonomy the diocese exercises in its decision to aid the schools, and in determining the nature of the aid.)

1. **Funds controlled directly by diocesan authorities:** Some dioceses have directed that the proceeds from special investment funds, or from revenue-generating diocesan enterprises be allocated for the support of inner-city schools. For example, in the late 1940s Philadelphia directed that a school serving the Chinese community be supported from the collection box of a center city chapel. Chicago, in recent years, has directed that the proceeds from investment funds be used to support inner-city schools. In most dioceses, the chief administrator (bishop or archbishop) has assigned a portion of the central income to the support of inner-city schools. Frequently, these funds have been reallocated from other activities supported by the diocese, such as seminaries, orphanages, and special charitable projects. In some cases, there is no real loss to the projects deprived of the funds: in the case of the seminaries because of a decline in vocations, or in the case of orphanages because of changes in public laws which reduce the number of institutionalized children and increase public funding. In other cases, dioceses have had to starve projects deemed not as vital, such as central educational television stations. Some chief administrators may have actually spent the capital set aside for investment purposes in helping to subsidize inner-city schools. However, we lack sufficient information about the sources of the diocesan funds spent on inner-city schools to determine this.

2. **Inter-parish transfers directed by the diocese:** In spending centrally controlled funds, the dioceses can act without consultation or approval of the parishes. In Los Angeles, for example, the

archbishop met privately with a pastor and provided him with funds to cover his inner-city-school-generated deficit in such a way that the parish did not have to report an official deficit. Its books were balanced. The archbishop and pastor dealt privately. However, in directing that inter-parish transfers be used to support inner-city schools, dioceses rely in varying degrees on the approval of the donor-parishes, for their voluntary cooperation is involved. The more the success of the effort depends on the cooperation of the laity, the more the chief diocesan administrator must make public his efforts, and actively seek out participation and shared responsibility.

Dioceses have made inner-city parish loans to cover the operating deficits of the parish. A typical parish spends 70% of its income on its school, and inner-city parishes often spend more, so that most of the loan proceeds went to cover school-generated deficits. In the late 1960s, the archdiocese of Chicago made loans totaling $5.6 million to subsidize inner-city parishes that have not even made interest payments on the loans. The principal is uncollectible. The loans will have to be written off, and the archdiocese will have expended a substantial proportion of its capital reserves on the operating expenses of the inner-city schools, *without anticipating that it was providing such an immense subsidy.* We do not know the number of dioceses that have aided inner-city schools through loans, but informal interviews indicate that most dioceses gave at least some such aid.

The funds loaned out were assembled by more solvent parishes, or by inner-city parishes in more solvent times, as building funds or other capital reserve funds, and were banked with diocesan officials. (This practice of central banking appears normal in dioceses where the chief administrator has the legal status of *corporation sole*, i.e., owns the assets of the church in his person.) Thus, the diocesan officials, however unwittingly, effected a subsidy of inner-city schools out of the capital accounts of wealthier parishes. The record suggests, but we do not know for certain, that many wealthier parishes have uncollectible credits on diocesan books. The practice may have imposed serious costs on the dioceses and parishes, because it may have prevented growing parishes in the outer-urban or suburban areas from building or expanding their schools. On paper, the parishes should be able to build their schools, but in fact the dioceses cannot finance them. Most dioceses have imposed a moratorium on building new schools for several years. We suspect there is a connection between the depletion of the capital accounts and the decision not to build schools in the suburban areas. The practice may have an important long-run consequence that will increase the difficulty of funding inner-city schools (which we shall discuss in a later chapter in greater detail): the church may be forced to ask wealthier parishes without schools of their own to subsidize inner-city schools.

The total value of uncollectible loans cannot readily be summed, since most records are not public. Projecting from the Chicago experience, we guess the total subsidy through defaulting loans will approach $50 million.

Dioceses have taxed or collected money from wealthier parishes to redistribute to parishes with schools in danger of failing. They have provided direct subsidies to the school budgets (usually giving special boards responsibility for determining the allocation) or indirect subsidy to the schools by support for the parish budget. Rarely do dioceses count the aid to the parishes as aid to inner-city schools. Often this aid goes directly from the chancery to the pastor, by-passing the diocesan education office.

The acknowledged subsidies are substantial. In Chicago they equal 2.3% of all parish income, amounting to about $20 million in the six years from 1971 to 1977. St. Louis, Detroit, New York, Brooklyn, and other dioceses have attempted this redistribution. We do not have adequate descriptions of the plans and approaches of each of the dioceses, nor of the size of their efforts.

Dioceses have joined parishes together under various programs, called "clustering" in Brooklyn where the linkage is quite close and formal, and "twinning" in Chicago where the linkage is much more variable and informal. These programs have met with varying degrees of success. The amount of redistribution through them has not been calculated by the diocese involved.

3. **Funds from non-diocesan sources, including parish funds not administered by the dioceses:** Inner-city schools are aided by several non-diocesan sources. Several subsidies involve non-renewable funds, such as accrued parish savings, or rely on dwindling organizational resources, such as the bank accounts of teaching orders. As these outside sources fail, dioceses will have to increase substantially their level of subsidy simply to stay even with present, inadequate levels.

Teaching orders subsidize Catholic schools. They do so directly, through their assumption of specific school costs and direct grants to the schools, and indirectly, through their provision of teaching services in exchange for subsistence incomes. Either the parish or the orders subsidize schools by providing housing and other necessities for religious teachers (and in some cases, for lay teachers). Because these costs are rarely accounted to the school, they are rarely counted as education subsidies. NCEA calculates that these subsidies are worth about $60 per pupil in Catholic elementary schools, but it does not include subsidies from lay teachers who work at below-market salaries.

Subsidies from religious orders have dropped dramatically in the past seven years and must be replaced by the diocese. Since 1970, Catholic elementary schools have lost 48%, and high schools 59%, of their religious teachers. The figures do not allow us to know the percent decline of religious in inner-city schools. Our own survey suggests, however, that inner-city schools have lost disproportionate numbers of religious.

Parishes provide two forms of subsidy that are not directed by diocesan authorities: direct subsidy of operating expenses out of parish-controlled reserve and savings accounts, and the provision of overhead services and expenses without charge to the school. Diocesan loans to inner-city school begin *only after parishes have spent their own reserves.*

In Philadelphia and similar dioceses where parishes retained greater autonomy than *corporation sole* dioceses like Chicago, parishes can bank their own funds for building funds or other reserves. When their inner-city parishes were younger and supported by large Catholic ethnic populations, they often built up substantial bank accounts. The Philadelphia archdiocese found virtually all its inner-city schools living on rapidly shrinking bank accounts. The parish schools continued to charge little or no tuition long after the number of active parishioners had dropped to levels too low to support the schools through church contributions. These parishes have almost consumed their capital reserves.

Even in Chicago, where the parish banks are located at the archdiocesan treasury, the parishes rely on accumulated savings before seeking loans from the archdiocese. We do not know the amount of capital invested in the operating expenses of inner-city schools from these sources. How many schools in changing neighborhoods, schools that are becoming inner-city schools, are living off capital savings? We do not know how much greater the financial needs of these schools will be in the near future, as savings run out.

Parishes provide some direct subsidy of their schools from current parish income. In most parishes the schools consume 70% of parish revenues. Conversely, Catholic schools receive on average 40% of their income from parish subsidies, and the rest from tuition, contributions and other sources. Unless the inner-city parish serves an ethnic Catholic population, the church typically has too few members to raise sufficient income to contribute to the school's support.

Most Catholic parishes give cash subsidy to the schools, and also offer in-kind aid, which they rarely account as an educational cost. Sometimes this aid can be major. For example, parishes commonly retire capital costs of the schools, (e.g., for construction and remodeling), through parish, not school, income. Parishes almost never calculate the school's *pro rata* share of the cost of the parish administrator's time, and routinely supply substantial overhead services without charging the school. Most parishes provide janitorial services, insurance for the school and grounds, maintenance and landscaping free of charge to the school. Many even provide the school with heat and electricity free of charge. Experience in the East has shown these hidden subsidies to be worth an additional $250 per pupil, exclusive of real capital investment subsidies and the value of the parish-administrator's time. These extra costs are clearly dependent on the regional economy (they will be much higher in Alaska, for example), on age and condition of the school plant, on its size and complexity, and other factors. As inner-city parish resources shrink, and overhead expenses rise, the parish will cut back on these subsidies. In the extreme case of one large Chicago inner-city parish, the school may be forced to subsidize the parish.

Total value of subsidies. In the absence of comprehensive, systematically collected information, we can make a reasonable projection of the total subsidy the church has supplied its inner-city schools in the past ten years. Based on the practice in Chicago, and on information from about 20 other dioceses gathered in the course of recent interviews, we estimate that the annual Catholic subsidy of inner-city schools—funds for current operating and capital expenses which exceed current parish and school income—has totalled about $100 million for the past ten years, or almost $1 billion in the decade. Subsidies given at the parish level, in the form of contributed services or school costs charged to the parish and not to the schools, approximately equal this amount. Total subsidies of inner-city schools by the church equals about 5% of the total Catholic education budget. NCEA has offered a much lower figure, 1% for the 1970-73 period, but that figure counts only transfers acknowledged by the parishes.

Despite the magnitude of the subsidy effort, inner-city Catholic schools have been forced to close, and dioceses have reached their financial limits. Chicago, Brooklyn, and New York City have cut the average subsidy to their schools in the past year, in part because more parishes have needed subsidy, in part because the dioceses have not been able to sustain their levels of subsidy in the face of declining incomes. Other dioceses have experienced the same squeeze on their subsidy programs, but we do not know to what extent. In any case, most observers believe the hidden well of parish reserves is drying up. These reserves cannot continue to support the schools.

Although sometimes necessary in an emergency, it is rarely wise to spend capital reserves for operating expenses, but that has been done to an alarming extent at the diocesan and parish levels. The church must solve the problem of financing the inner-city schools by analyzing the causes of the problem, and by making provision that the schools operate off income, not savings. Many dioceses have cut adrift schools which cannot show the possibility of operating off income. Cutting adrift inner-city Catholic schools is tantamount to closing them. There are other choices, although quite clearly all require some reorganization of the parish structure. For as we shall see in the next chapter, the problem of financing inner-city Catholic schools stems from the fact that Catholic schools are financed by their parishes, and in the inner-city, the parishes are too poor or have too few members, to support them.

Questions for Research

In this chapter, we identified a number of information-gaps which have prevented the church from recognizing the problem it faces with inner-city schools.

Foremost, the church must begin to collect information about the level of minority enrollments in each diocese, population trends in its urban parishes, number of students enrolled in school with annual deficits, and the efforts each diocese has made to eliminate the deficits. Up to this time, each diocese has reinvented the wheel in attempting to define its problem with inner-city schools and devise a solution. It is time for a national study which would examine in detail, and in a disinterested fashion, the advantages and liabilities of each of the approaches already attempted. Decent statistics about the number of inner-city schools which have closed must be developed. Information on the kinds of problems the schools will face in the next five years is extremely important if the church is ever to advance its policy-making abilities to the stage where it can correct problems before their full effects are felt.

Chart 1A

CHANGE IN PERCENTAGE OF CATHOLIC STUDENTS ENROLLED IN CATHOLIC SCHOOLS, BY ETHNICITY, 1970-77

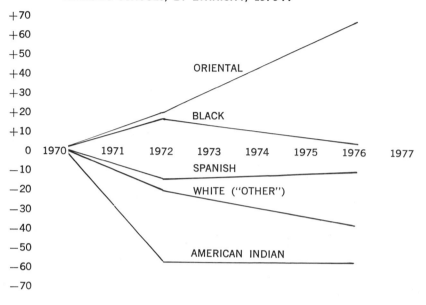

Source: NCEA data bank.

PERCENT OF PERSONS BORN CATHOLIC BY ETHNIC GROUP,* AND PERCENT OF GROUP MEMBERS ATTENDING CATHOLIC SCHOOLS, 1965

Ethnic Group	% of Catholics by Ethnicity	% of Group Attending Only Catholic Schools	% of Group Attending Some Catholic Schools
Italian	20	8	31
Irish	18	30	77
German	17	21	64
Polish	10	22	77
French	10	34	78
Eastern European	9	13	52
English	6	20	57
Spanish	5	4	22
Other	4	7	45
	N=1,840	N=1,852	N=1,852

* Father's ethnicity controls

Source: *The Education of Catholic Americans*, Table 2.6 and Table 2.14.

Notes on Sources for Chapter 1

Sources for the statistical information used in this chapter:

U.S. Dept. of Health, Education, and Welfare, Office of Education, Statistics of Non-Public Elementary and Secondary Schools, 1970-71 (DHEW Publication No. (OE) 74-11420).

U.S., DHEW, National Center for Education Statistics, *Condition of Education, 1976,* (USGPO No. 017-080-01521-8).

National Center for Education Statistics, *Condition of Education, 1977* (USGPO No. 017-080-01678-8).

National Catholic Education Association Data Bank, *U.S. Catholic Schools, 1970-1977,* (NCEA: Washington, D.C. annual).

U.S. Dept. of Commerce, Bureau of Census, *Spring 1976 Survey of Income and Education,* Series P-60, Nos. 108-112, *Consumer Income* (USGPO, June, 1978).

Andrew Greeley and Peter Rossi, *The Education of Catholic Americans,* (Chicago: Aldine Publishing Co., 1966).

Information on finances of the Catholic school systems was obtained in the course of research financed by the National Institute of Education and the Office of Education.

CHAPTER 2

THE PROBLEMS OF INNER-CITY SCHOOLS

Why are Catholic inner-city schools in such difficulty? In the past, even poor parishes could build and support a school. Why are today's inner-city parishes unable to support existing schools? Is it a change in the nation's social or economic life that makes supporting private schools more difficult for lower-income families today? Is it a change in the Church? Or are inner-city schools today different from the Catholic schools that successfully served lower-income immigrants in the past?

Social, Economic and Political Causes of the Crisis Facing Inner-City Schools

The problems facing inner-city schools to close originate not in the school, but in the community. Many originate in the economic and political structure of our society and are far beyond the ability of the schools to correct. State or federal governments are not likely to help schools survive the problems—important as inner-city Catholic schools are to the public interest—because their existing policies have in part created the problems. This is not to say the schools cannot survive, but only that they cannot survive if they continue to operate as they have in the past. They must adapt to the new situations in which they find themselves.

The problems facing the inner-city Catholic schools confront all public and private institutions and individuals who attempt to serve the needs of the inner-city: public schools, churches, service organizations like the YMCA, businesses, and landlords. At root, the problems are caused by the increasing concentration of the poor in inner-cities and the simultaneous depopulation of the area (as residential buildings deteriorate, burn, or are abandoned, or as families mature and are not replaced by younger families). A host of economic, technological, social and legal pressures combine to encourage wealthier families to put ever-increasing distances between themselves and the poor, who remain locked in the aging inner-city areas. Left with only the poor, the institutions are no longer self-supporting.

Public laws encourage—almost require—this pattern of development. Federal internal revenue, housing, transportation, and welfare policies are particularly responsible, as are state municipal incorporation laws that permit suburbanites to establish upper-income governmental enclaves, as well as taxation, education, and zoning laws. For example, the federal government greatly influences the location of home mortgages through the FHA and VA mortgage guarantee and subsidy programs, by controlling the practices of the Federal National Mortgage Association and Federal Savings and Loan Insurance Corporation. For all practical purposes, the federal government has required participating lenders to give mortgages only to new construction outside the central city, thus denying cities the capital needed to rehabilitate housing stock.

As if this were not enough, the internal revenue codes give enormous tax benefits to families purchasing new homes outside the city, especially when compared to those living in older, unmortgaged homes in the city or in city apartments. The tax benefits can halve the effective housing costs for suburban home owners and, when combined with the education benefits available in the suburbs, force wealthy families to relocate. The wealthier the family, the greater its tax incentive to leave the city.

Families of even modest income can live great distances from the center city because, beginning in the 1950s, the federal highway program subsidized the construction of arterial highways around center cities, and eventually permitted places of work to relocate—with substantial advantages—far from the central city. Thus, the center city was deprived of its middle class and a great number of jobs.

Simultaneously, federal and state welfare policies, through reliance on local financing of welfare costs and the granting of local options in support levels and the kinds of welfare problems covered, created a system which deprives public assistance recipients of most or all their benefits if they move from the central city. These federal policies, combined with suburban zoning policies which made the construction of low-cost housing virtually impossible and federal urban renewal policies which permitted suburban and county governments to veto construction of public housing within their jurisdictions, insured that lower-income families would be locked into inner-cities.

These laws have had a double effect on inner-city areas. They have driven investment capital out of the city *directly* by regulating home mortgages, and *indirectly* by encouraging income groups which invest and attract investment to leave the city. This process is particularly devastating for the inner-city because such areas are reaching the advanced stages of natural physical decay, and require reinvestment to prevent abandonment and destruction. Massive abandonment of inner-city areas has already occurred in large midwestern and eastern cities.

The public laws were not designed to create these problems for the inner-city, but to benefit the public—or some section of the public. The laws permitting deduction of home mortgage interest expenses, for example, were designed to stimulate single-family home construction, and thereby increase construction jobs and stimulate the economy. The highway program was designed to relieve congestion, increase safety, and open up the country-side to development. Despite their intended benefits, however, the laws have damaged the inner-city and its public institutions, including Catholic schools. The principal damaging problems include the following:

1. The gradual aging of inner-city populations and facilities, caused by a failure to reinvest in housing and businesses in the area and the resulting lack of jobs.

2. A consequent depopulation, as young people move else-where to start their families because of the absence of adequate housing and as housing is abandoned for lack of financing to remedy problems caused by aging. Both effects deprive the schools of students and the parishes of income from young working families, of support from local businesses (which parishes and schools often receive), and of ability to raise capital for rehabilitation. In some places, such as Chicago's South Side or New York's South Bronx, the depopulation is absolute—Catholic schools are surrounded by blocks of rubble. Most inner-city neighborhoods suffer less from depopulation than from the concentration of poor within their areas, as wealthier families are drawn away.

3. A rapid change in ethnic composition of the neighborhood, as entire ethnic communities move out and are replaced by even poorer newcomers. In some cases, the newcomers are not actually poorer, but are perceived by residents as of lower social status, such as blacks and some Latino groups. The rapid change of a high proportion of residents weakens the social organization of a Catholic parish and its ability to support a school in a lower-income neighborhood.

Where the Catholic school is the only building standing in its neighborhood, there is little point to saving it. Whatever the school does, the neighborhood conditions have defeated it. Few Catholic schools face that situation. Even when their neighborhoods are greatly depopulated, they can often extend the bounds of their attendance area or eliminate the attendance area altogether. They can combine forces with other Catholic schools nearby, consolidating for efficiency. The most significant ethnic changes in the inner-cities in the past twenty years have been the increase in the proportion of blacks and, more recently, of Latinos. Both these populations present similar problems for inner-city schools because they have much lower proportions of active Catholics than the departing ethnic groups, making it more difficult to support the schools by the traditional American Catholic approach of parish funds. The schools and the dioceses can adapt to the new situation, and many have made substantial attempts to change their organizational structure—some more successfully than others. Generally, inner-city Catholic schools have done too little, too late. The schools are in trouble, not because the church changed its organization, but because it failed to change as quickly as it should have. With few exceptions, elementary schools belong to parishes, and in discussing the way dioceses govern and finance their elementary schools, we are necessarily describing how and to what extent diocesan officials control parish activities. The reader who is unfamiliar with the Catholic system should note: there is no such thing as *the* approach dioceses take with their parishes, or *the* approach diocesan education departments take with the schools. The U.S. Catholic Church is a confederation of semi-autonomous dioceses, formally of equal stature. Dioceses differ in their organizational and political approach to the operation of parishes and schools because of accidents in the historical development of the diocese, requirements of state laws regulating churches and other non-profit organizations, or directives of the recent or current bishop or archbishop.

Territorial Parish Organization of the Diocese

The basic organizational principle is territorial, with the U.S. divided into dioceses and the dioceses into parishes. Diocesan and parish membership is determined by residence, not selective affiliation. (At the end of the nineteenth century, the bishops considered an approach more akin to that employed in Protestant churches, where affiliation with a parish is selective. Parishes would have served ethnic groups, with an Italian parish, an Irish parish, a black parish, and a Polish parish all serving residents of the same territory. Some vestiges of this approach continue to exist in Eastern and Midwestern dioceses.)

In a territorially organized system, political controls are more centralized than they are in one organized by parishioners' selective affiliation with the parish. Parish administrators can be more easily reassigned in the former system, and finances can be more centrally controlled. In a selectively organized parish—and some Orthodox Greek Catholic churches present examples—

—the parishioners may decide to sell the old church property and physically relocate the church. The parish savings account for building fund, reserve funds, etc. remains with the people and not with the old building. In a territorially organized parish, however, the accounts of the parish remain with the building, and the building remains the parish seat—unless the bishop decides to reorganize his diocese. Because parishioners are members of a parish by residence, they enter and leave the parish. Even if all parishioners leave at the same time, the parish remains for the incoming group of residents, and any savings that former parishioners accrued are left for the newcomers. This imposes little hardship on individual Catholics, however, since they find it easy to join a new parish whenever they relocate, and, in most areas, find church and school facilities awaiting them.

Territorial organization, the patterns of residential mobility of the American population in recent years, and the increasing impoverishment of the inner-city have produced the church's inner-city schools. The church has schools in areas that it would not necessarily choose today because they are located in parishes which are too poor or have too few Catholics to support them. On the one hand, the church's territorial organization has benefited inner-cities because it has made the church more reluctant to pull its investments and assets out of the inner-city than it would be under a selective parish organizational approach. But the territorial approach also causes trouble. Parishes which cannot build schools can rarely support them without aid. Where does responsibility for the existing inner-city schools rest when the parish cannot support them? It would seem to rest with the diocese. Dioceses, in varying degrees, control all parish assets, and would therefore appear to be quite wealthy. In the extreme case—dioceses like Chicago or Boston—the parish assets are accounted as belonging to the Church as a *corporation sole* under state laws. Consequently, all the assets of the parishes and diocese are unified in a single organization, and owned as the personal property of the bishop or archbishop. In such dioceses, parishes frequently do not control separate bank accounts, but bank all money with the diocesan central bank, where central authorities have greater control over its use. It is even possible for the central authorities to borrow from commercial banks and put up parish assets as security for the loan. In other words, they can mortgage the diocese—as they reportedly have done in Boston. In other dioceses, parishes retain greater control over their funds, sometimes maintaining their own bank accounts. Even in these parishes, funds remain with the parish when parishioners move to other sections of the diocese.

The picture of centralized control of church assets leads us to believe that diocesan officials can simply decide to spend church money to support inner-city schools. Diocesan officials can make the decision formally, but not practically—not without obtaining the assent of the parishioners who contribute the money.

Only a small portion of the dioceses' operating income comes from return on invested assets; almost all comes from current contributions from parishioners. The largest portion of these contributions supports the parish in which the members reside; a smaller portion is sent from the parish to the diocese to underwrite its expenses. Because revenues come from voluntary contributions, church officials must be even more sensitive to the concerns of church members than public officials are to the concerns of taxpayers. Taxpayers, after all, are required by law to pay taxes. Dissatisfied parishioners do not contribute.

Diocesan authorities are not perfectly free to allocate money to inner-city parishes, but must get parishioners of solvent parishes to agree to contribute. Diocesan authorities have some leeway, because a low level of taxation of the parishes is not likely to become an issue, nor spark opposition, and can be carried out without the active approval of the contributing parishioners. Central diocesan offices reportedly operate at low levels of parish taxation, receiving only 5% to 10% of parish receipts for central diocesan purposes. But higher levels of taxation on the parishes, especially when identifiably related to a single diocesan activity—such as its effort to finance inner-city schools —may well alter the traditional "independence" of diocesan authorities. The real test of autonomous centralized authority is whether central officials can make and carry out plans without consulting the parishes; the most severe test comes when parish administrators or members actively oppose the plans. By this test, most decisions affecting Catholic parishes and their schools appear to be made at the parish level. Central authorities actively control only a small portion of funds. This is not to say the central authorities of the church are weak, or unimportant; they establish the broad strategies the church in America follows. But within that framework, there is substantial discretion and autonomy for the parishes. This pattern is reflected in the schools: one can legitimately question whether there is any Catholic school *system* in any diocese. Certainly there is none comparable to the public school systems. The more vigorous the definition of "system," with its implications of interdependency and centralized, rational control, the less true it is that any Catholic school system exists.

Normal parish governance and finance: In general, Catholic dioceses have moved from a system of parish financing of parish schools to a system of financing schools with a combination of parish funds and school tuitions. Today, 60-70% of all school revenues come from tuition, 30-40% from parish subsidy. In the past, about 80% of parish income went to the school, and that percentage does not appear to have changed significantly. The total contributions to the parish have dropped as the support of the schools has become less and less a parish responsibility.

Dioceses have traditionally had nothing to do with the policies guiding the financing of parish schools. The dioceses do make some rules, such as, "No Catholic student should be deprived of a Catholic education because his or her parents cannot afford tuition at the parish school." Normally, these rules are only the articulation of rules the parishes are already following. Recalcitrant parishes are ignored.

In most dioceses, the central office characterizes itself as a resource center, available to help at the request of the parish. It suggests what parish schools might do, helps them make changes it believes in, and sets or recommends policies it thinks they should follow. It does not monitor, and has no enforcement mechanism.

The diocese can attempt to mandate some changes. Chicago, for example, tried to get all parish schools to pay lay teachers salaries according to an archdiocesan schedule; to put the teacher pension plan on a reasonable footing; to budget the school separately from the church; and to specify the subsidy the parish gives its school. Even today, all Chicago parishes do not follow these mandates. Over the years, the archdiocesan department of education has gradually stopped using the terms, "central directives" or "rules," and substituted the terms, "suggestions" or "guidelines." When the department of education took upon itself the review of requests for financial aid from the schools, however, it was able to require those schools to follow its budgeting format.

The diocesan department of education is most often funded through a head tax every school pays for each of its students. In return for the funding, the schools expect the central office to provide services that more than offset the tax. Chicago meets this objective by providing a central purchasing service, which saves schools substantial amounts of money; a centralized pension program; some central bookkeeping services; centralized educational television courses; and trouble-shooting and coordination of state and federal aid programs.

31

In the normal parish, funding the schools begins with the parents and flows outward to the diocese. The diocese does not collect the money and return it to the parishes, nor do the parents directly pay the diocese. The financial system of the diocese resembles more a political *confederation* than it does the U.S. *federal* system. However, most dioceses are forced to become the source of funds for some of their inner-city parishes. Unlike the federal government, the diocese cannot "tax" its members directly but must work through its local governments, the parishes. *Dioceses act differently toward the schools they subsidize:* The central office gains sanctions and responsibilities, and the aided parishes lose a measure of independence. As a general rule, inner-city schools must obey more central directives than totally self-sufficient schools in the same diocese.

The Special Problems of Inner-City Parish Schools: Decline in Income

The territorial organization of the church limits the ability of diocesan officials to redistribute church income to serve-inner-city needs. It also creates an additional problem. We noted that the church maintained its assets in the inner-city area, but we were referring only to buildings and bank accounts. The church is not a foundation with most of its assets invested in interest-bearing accounts. Its assets are primarily buildings—churches, schools, orphanages, and the like. Their income is derived principally from donations. The greatest income-producing asset of a parish is not the church building, but the parishioner who contributes to the church. When a parishioner relocates, some of the parish income goes with him or her. In normal situations, the relocating parishioner will be replaced by another, and the income of the parish will, on the average, be maintained. In a changing neighborhood, especially in the inner city, the incoming resident is likely to be a non-Catholic or an inactive member of the parish. In the inner city there may be no incoming resident; a house may be abandoned or destroyed. The parish has no way of increasing its income.

When parish revenues decline as the result of neighborhood change, a diocese faces three choices. It can continue to staff and finance its insolvent inner-city parishes; consolidate parishes (or schools, the major financial burden of inner-city parishes); or close the parish and redivide the territory among nearby parishes. Most dioceses employ all three approaches, as the situation of each inner-city parish and school warrants. The last two options, which are practical solutions to immediate financial difficulties, preserve the parish-based revenue structure of the diocese, but create serious organizational problems as parishes with different memberships and staffs—each with its own social organization, privileges and traditions—try to merge. Decisions to consolidate or close and reassign the territory to several parishes are often tantamount to the church's withdrawing from the area altogether, because staff is spread too thin to maintain contact with parishioners. However, if the diocese decides to finance inner-city schools and parishes directly, the normal financial arrangements between parish and diocese are reversed.

Loss of Parish Autonomy

Most dioceses have had some experience in financing parishes when they began new ones or established missions. Financing inner-city parishes and schools is different. New parishes become self-sustaining shortly after being funded. But a diocese does not expect missions to support themselves in the near future, and makes other provisions for their financing, releasing the mission staff for more pastoral work. Consequently, dioceses do not support significant numbers of missions, for they are not organized to redistribute parish funds on a large scale. Dioceses expect that even missions will become normal parishes, making the change from dependency on outside support and direction to self-support and self-direction. Inner-city parishes and their schools are moving in the opposite direction. Is there any prospect that these parishes and schools can again become independent, relying on their own resources? Can a mission approach be applied to inner-city parishes as a guide to supporting the parishes and their schools, and showing a way to eventual self-sufficiency?

Mission schools are founded and financed by outsiders who retain control of the basic decisions affecting the mission school. The mission school embraces the belief, in principle if not in practice, that even the adults of the community are ignorant of what the school is trying to teach and are therefore incapable of self-direction. American mission schools have traditionally served people who: (1) live at subsistence level; (2) are usually non-Catholics; and (3) live within a culture greatly different from the dominant American culture. Thus, mission schools serving American Indians in Maine, New Mexico, Alaska, or elsewhere are serving a people culturally and economically isolated from the mainstream of American life. Given their dependency on outsiders, mission schools could become extremely authoritarian and paternalistic. That tendency is moderated, however, by the mission's need for acceptance from the people it serves—the

33

mission can succeed only if the people want what it offers. Missions traditionally adopt the community's cultural symbols and activities in their educational efforts. They try to create a self-sufficient, Catholic community that produces is own staff, sets its own directions, and finances its own operation—in other words, a parish. Not surprisingly, Catholic mission schools are among the most militant supporters of indigenous tribal culture in the American Indian territories.

Inner-city parishes resemble mission parishes in a number of respects. Inner-city schools often enroll high percentages of non-Catholics, as mission schools almost always do, and the people they serve are almost always poor and of a minority race or culture. There are also several differences. Mission schools traditionally seek converts, while parish schools have no such tradition. Mission schools typically serve residents of remote areas where the minority culture can be accommodated and nurtured without causing undue alarm to those funding the mission effort, where there is a salutory distance between those giving the money and the services they are funding. In the inner-city, the minority culture rubs against the dominant culture, and those providing the funds are constant witnesses to the efforts of the minority culture to assert its independence. The authorities responsible for the use of the funds are therefore held more closely accountable by those contributing, than are the mission schools. In the mission experience there were fewer political repercussions that would be expected if the mission model were applied to inner-city schools.

Inheriting the Shell of a Parish

Political considerations aside, diocesan experience with mission schools is not a good guide for a solution to inner-city school problems. The principal cause of inner-city problems is a population declining in numbers and income, that frequently changes its ethnic and religious characteristics. Missions do not experience this change. To stop the population decline, there is little the church can do, apart from encouraging parish administrators to become politically active in order to force changes in public policies that would help stabilize inner-city neighborhoods.

A significant amount of the financial strain suffered by inner-city parishes and their schools results from parishes' difficulties in adjusting to the rapid ethnic changes in their neighborhoods. True, the resources of the neighborhood are declining, but the parish resources typically decline disproportionately because the inner-city parish has trouble organizing new residents to support the parish and its school. Let us review the principal strains caused by neighborhood ethnic, economic and racial changes that make organization of the parish more difficult:

(1) **Facilities:** In earlier periods, when many inner-city neighborhoods had heavily Catholic populations, parishes built immense facilities. Given a sufficient number of Catholics, even a parish frequently of very low-income workers could build a large impressive church and school. Today, because the groups moving into these areas are usually non-Catholic or inactive Catholics, the typical inner-city parish is overbuilt. For example, a former Irish parish on the South side of Chicago was an affluent, solidly Catholic neighborhood in the first part of the century. The parish was large and was able to cover a city block with a magnificent neo-Gothic church, a rectory, a convent, and several school buildings. Today the parish is all black. At least 60% of the school's 1,300 students are non-Catholics, and the parish counts fewer than 800 members, many of them on pension incomes. The parish has a hard time paying the energy bill for the *church*, and has no resources for the school.

An inner-city parish benefits from the buildings left behind by previous parishioners. Normally, when a diocese establishes a new parish, a church is built only when parishioners are no longer willing to crowd into a public school auditorium, or to borrow the facilities of a neighboring Protestant or Catholic church. The church building is usually built small, often as a basement for a larger structure or as the auditorium of what will become the school. It is enlarged only when parishioners become tired of standing through Sunday masses. A school is built only when enough families request one, and frequently new schools have waiting lists even for children of parishioners. New residents in inner-city parishes avoid all of this: they find a built-up parish waiting for them.

Ironically, the very fact that the parish does not have to build facilities can cause great difficulties with its organization. Parish administrators must organize their parishioners to help and support the parish. Building new facilities is a means of nurturing the social organization of the parish, of spotting leaders, of working out the mechanics of the parish's organization, of teaching both administrators and parishioners to share responsibilities, of building up trust. *Not* having to experience the inconvenience of the crowded auditorium, *not* having encountered and gradually solved small problems means that the first problems the new parishioners encounter are likely to be major ones. All organizations learn by trial and error. The inner-city parish may have to build up its organization while facing major crises, such as the financial collapse of the school, rather than the relatively minor questions faced by less well-developed parishes.

Financial and organizational problems aside, a well developed parish still presents difficulties to incoming ethnics. Parish churches are typically designed to fit the traditions of the ethnic group that constructed them, and these traditions are likely to be foreign to the new group. The design of the church helps bind the parish closer to the families and to traditions extending back to the old country. Frequently, the parish employed priests and nuns who knew the language, traditions, and even the former villages and neighborhoods of immigrant parishioners. The staff was selected to fit the ethnicity of the parishioners; the buildings were constructed to fit their traditions, all of which are foreign to the new ethnic group. Although the parish staff and iconography can change, changes are difficult and take time. The church does not have sufficient staff familiar with the traditions of black families, nor has the American church developed an iconography that connects it closely to the traditions of black Americans. It is more difficult to change the existing ethnic identity of a parish than to devlop a new parish.

(2) **Parish funds:** The former parishioners typically leave building, improvement or reserve funds behind, which the succeeding inner-city parish can use to pay operating deficits. The reserve funds are a great advantage and can help the parish through its most difficult period. However, they can also allow it to operate inefficiently and to postpone its own needs. For example, the full pressure of the cost of maintaining the large buildings may become obvious to parishioners only when the reserve funds have been spent.

(3) **Governing approaches:** Finally, the old parishioners leave behind an approach to running the parish that may or may not be suitable to the newcomers. The composition of the parish may change from business persons and professionals to clerical and blue-collar workers, from highly educated and experienced managers to workers with low-level educational and managerial skills. In the original parish (after 1965), a parish council may have taken care of the books, planned needs, run the school, etc. Should the same structure be used for the newcomers? What if the newcomers are immigrants who speak little English? Is the parish best served by leaving control of important functions, such as budgeting and tuition collection, in the hands of lay leaders? In some parishes, the election of lay leaders is an important and useful activity. Would it be appropriate if most parishioners were

Appalachian whites, whose individualism runs so strong that they will often refuse to select or—if they do select—to follow a leader? In the case of Appalachian whites, or non-Catholic blacks, or Latinos an even more serious problem occurs. In a normal parish, traditionally, Mass and other regular meetings between the pastor or parish administrators and the parishioners permitted a communication between those formally making decisions affecting the parish, and its members. In parishes where there are few active Catholics, this communication does not exist. The problem is especially great when parish or diocesan decisions affect an inner-city school attended by large numbers of non-Catholics. Take for example a decision to close the school because it cannot be financed. In a typical Catholic parish, the parishioners would be well aware of the problems leading to the closing, and would feel a responsibility for them well before the time to close the school. They would, in a sense, be prepared for the school's closing. For non-Catholics there are no regular means for them to become involved in the decision. Typically, the church does not even obtain from non-Catholic parents the full amount of support they are capable of giving the school, for they are not made to feel responsible for its operation in the same way that Catholic parishioners are. There exists no regular channel by which non-Catholics, for whom the educational opportunity provided by inner-city schools is extremely important, to voice their concerns to the pastor, bishop or other officials responsible for the school's future. It is difficult under present structures for anyone to regard the claims of the non-Catholic parents as legitimate, in a technical sense. The bishop or pastor making the decision to close the school is not a public official, and does not need to consult with the public before making his decision.

Inner-city schools often belong to the *shells* of parishes, a parish which has buildings, staff, territory, and people living within its jurisdiction, but no organization of those people, no community. Schools in such parishes may not seem to help the parish, in the eyes of parish administrators. Pastors who decide to close inner-city schools often note that these schools no longer provide Catholic instruction, follow Catholic traditions, or have any Catholic students. They conclude that the school is not necessary to families in the parish—there are too few families to support it—and complain, or simply note, that the school staff has not embarked upon any mission effort to increase parish membership. Rarely do Catholic inner-city schools actively attempt to convert non-Catholics to increase parish membership.

The rift between inner-city parish and school, which can grow as the population of the school becomes increasingly non-

Catholic, is not healthy for either. Inner-city schools need the parish for political and financial reasons to help organize the neighborhood into a strong unit capable of defending itself against the urban forces causing neighborhood decline; and to subsidize the school so that it becomes financially independent, accommodates itself to parishioners' cultural needs, and enrolls more of the poorest members of the parish at no charge. The schools, if they are to survive, must help the parishes revive.

Patterns of Inner-City School Government and Finance

As a practical matter, Catholic leaders must develop ways to subsidize the operations of inner-city schools even before the task of rebuilding the parish is completed. It is particularly important that the problem of integrating non-Catholics into the governance and finance of these schools be solved. One way to begin is by summarizing and assessing the kinds of parish governmental and financing approaches which have been tried in the inner city. The church lacks systematic data on how its parishes operate, and cannot say which forms have the greater chance of success in the inner-city, and under what conditions. We can begin that assessment by describing the types of existing approaches.

Inner-city school governance: The formal arrangements determining how schools are governed and who does the governing are critical for inner-city schools, especially for schools with large percentages of non-Catholic parents. In all inner-city schools, the problem is not so much how to please parents as it is how to get the most effort and commitment from them. Inner-city schools do not give parents a role in governing the schools because they have some fundamental right to it, but because parent involvement makes the school more effective and increases its chances for survival.* Inner-city schools require tremendous amounts of free labor from their supporters to replace income they cannot obtain. The school's governance arrangements strongly affect parents' willingness to volunteer to work for the school. Parents' investment of their own time and labor in the school has an added benefit: it gives them a strong sense of having invested in the school, and having a personal stake in its achievements.

---

* Catholic inner-city schools must be cautious of the rhetoric of local control, not because local control is damaging to the schools, but because they have already reached most of the objectives the "local control" movement is attempting to reach in public schools and because local control rhetoric can alienate their key supporters.

38

Even when an inner-city school manages to obtain substantial direct parental support without formally improving the way it consults with parents, it will be forced eventually to make the change. When parents feel the school survives because of their efforts, they begin to feel they have a right to be consulted about decisions which affect it. The following example, drawn as a composite of case histories in Philadelphia, Chicago and New York, illustrates the difficulties that can develop when church administrators fail to recognize that they must consult those supporting the school.

In the course of three years, a parish of Slavic Catholics becomes 80% black. The blacks enroll in the parish school, but do not join the parish. The pastor is accustomed to making all the decisions about the school and announcing them in church. He is also used to paying all the school bills by a vest-pocket accounting system—he puts the money in one pocket and takes it out of another. As the parish changes, the church loses revenue, and the pastor can no longer pay the school's bills. He begins to spend the parish reserve fund, and the school begins to make greater use of parent volunteers to cut costs. The pastor realizes other neighboring parishes are having similar problems with their schools: the problem is that the school was built to serve twice the number of students who are enrolled. If he closes his school, and the students transfer to the neighboring parish, he will help that school to survive, and his own school's students will still receive a Catholic education. He announces his decision from the pulpit to close the school.

In a number of similar cases, teachers or parents rebelled against the pastor's decision. In Chicago, the central school board—set up by the archbishop to advise on diocesan education policy—backed the school personnel and the parents. The archbishop was forced to choose between the teacher-parent coalition and their pastor. The matter was no longer confined to pastor vs. non-Catholic parents, because other participants—lay leaders and religious teachers—had given their opinion.

In New York city, an outside group—CORE—led parents in demonstrations at diocesan school headquarters.

The lesson of this composite case is that those who support the school, and those whose needs the schools meet, should be involved in its governance, even if involvement is no more than information and consultation. The best guideline for involving each potential supporter in the operation of the schools seems to be: give each a voice in the school commensurate with his or her stake—don't give heavy responsibilities to those getting little benefit from the school. Do not ignore those to whom the school is important. A list of potential supporters of inner-city schools includes: the principal, lay and religious teachers, parents, pastor, parishioners, diocesan educational staff, diocesan secretary for education, the bishop or archbishop, community residents and people of the city. We find that each of these types of supporters are involved in existing inner-city schools in a number of different ways and use a variety of organizational devices. There are five distinct types of governance systems in inner-city schools.

1. **Patriarchal mission school:** Financial support comes from the outside—usually the diocese—as do basic decisions on how the support will be used. The pastor must be a strong leader who satisfies his superiors enough to encourage them to continue support. At the same time, he must also convince his teachers to support the school through their personal subsidy. Such a school is rarely directed by the parents.

2. **Collegial mission school:** The religious teaching order raises funds for the school at the school level. In this case, the order seeks more active support from parents and involves them in decisions about what the school will be doing. This approach makes the school more independent of central authorities.

3. **Patriarchal parish school:** The pastor is a figure of authority, but by consensus. He is "one of the people of the parish." Such a pastor often runs into difficulty in the inner-city because his approach to governance rests on establishing the sense of identity between himself, as chief decision-maker, and parents in the school. The identity functions in two directions: it puts the parents at ease with the pastor's decisions, even when they find his decisions unpleasant, such as a requirement that all parents attend monthly parent-teacher meetings or pay a fine; it permits the pastor to make decisions while taking into account his parishioners' concerns and needs. When the parish changes so rapidly that a pastor no longer knows its members, or when the parish has few Catholics, the patriarchal parish is in difficulty. The pastor is no longer "one of the people."

4. **Mixed forms:** Often the pastor shifts the chief responsibility for the school to the principal and teachers, but retains limited control over finances and religious education. Sometimes religious orders organize the school around a strong principal; sometimes they share responsibility by rotation. More frequently, the orders bring parents into the operation of the school by

having them set and collect tuition and advise on hiring and school policy.

5. **Parent-run school:** At the far extreme are parent-run schools. In some examples, inner-city Catholic school board elections are open to everyone in the neighborhood, and local neighborhood leaders are elected to serve on the board. The purpose of such a board is to build community support for the school and to encourage financial support from those who benefit from the schools, even though they have no children in them. The school boards must work with the teachers—religious or lay—who are the backbone of the school. Teachers' subsidy to the school, in the guise of long hours and low wages, gains them deference and authority in matters affecting the schools. Parent-run schools may operate totally independently of priests or religious teaching orders. In the extreme example of this type of school, the parents break the school's ties with the church.

Inner-city school financing: The financing arrangements for inner-city schools are clearer than their governance systems. There are only a few sources for the needed money.

1. **Parish subsidy and tuition:** The financing can come from the parish. Inner-city parishes with large Catholic populations can pay most school costs from parish revenues. Generally, financing will come from some combination of parish support and tuition. The fewer Catholics in the parish, the greater the importance of tuition to the school's budget. The more the school relies on parish subsidy, the greater the active role of the pastor in the school. The more the school relies on tuition, the greater the authority of the principal or parents.

Some inner-city schools try to pay all school bills with tuition. In these cases, the tuition costs sky-rocket. *The highest tuitions charged for parish elementary schools in the Catholic system are in inner-city schools.* The highest we found in 1975-76 in the largest Catholic systems was $1,700 per student at one Harlem school, but we found tuitions of $500-850 in almost every city. (Ninety percent of all Catholic elementary schools charged tuitions below $400 in 1975, but few inner-city schools relying on tuition could charge such low rates.) Collecting tuitions has become a great difficulty for parishes. One parish, which found that parents entrusted with delicate financial information were gossiping, had to disband the school board. Another parish found that the parents were extremely severe on parents (and even their children) who did not pay on time. Other parishes found, however, that parents refused to pay on time if the pastor or the

41

school handled the payments, but were never late when parents collected. Increasingly, parishes have been turning to parents to handle tuition collection because many teachers and religious think the task interferes with their professional duties. As parents assume the role, their responsibility for the school grows.

In parishes that give no support to the school, the school tends to be isolated from the parish. The pastor is often only cursorily informed of the school's activities and problems and is rarely asked to help. Antagonisms develop when the pastor, showing less concern for the school's problems than its administrator might, withdraws money from the school accounts to pay parish debts. Even parishes which do not directly subsidize their schools often pay substantial school expenses that are never properly accounted, such as maintenance, heating, insurance, and ground's upkeep. One inner-city school found that its parish paid about $300 per pupil in such subsidies.

2. **Diocesan subsidies:** Dioceses have tried to support inner-city schools in a number of ways. Initially, most dioceses allow inner-city parishes to spend accumulated parish funds on their operating deficits. Then the diocese makes loans, which it will subsequently be forced to write off, since they are made to cover operating expenses and will produce no revenue. The diocese then begins efforts to tax wealthier schools and parishes to support the inner-city parishes running deficits.

Under the support plans, a needy parish must submit a budget for the coming year showing all anticipated revenues, all expenses, and the amount of subsidy needed. The budget may be submitted to the superintendent of schools, the central school board, or the bishop's secretary for education. The budget proposals are reviewed, and the central board decides on the level of funds it can provide. In some cases, to stretch the funds as far as possible, the board will set a limit on support levels. In several dioceses, the archbishop requires schools to submit plans showing what steps they are taking to become self-support ing in a short period of time, because the diocese cannot and will not undertake permanent financing of operating expenses for the inner-city schools.

Dioceses have met with varied success in getting wealthy parishes to subsidize inner-city schools. Two notable failures include Detroit, where the wealthier parishes went on a "contribution strike" and forced the diocese to withdraw its order; and Brooklyn, where wealthier parishes flatly refused to share resources with poorer parishes. The matter has become more complex in recent times as lay boards have been established, especially in wealthier parishes, to control budgets and finances. Dioceses now have less influence and control over these boards.

Published data does not reveal the degree of success of diocesan efforts to obtain *voluntary* contributions from wealthy parishes. The Chicago archdiocese operates two aid programs: one financed through direct subscription, the other a "twinning" program in which two parishes determine resources they will share. In the past six years, the diocese has redistributed almost $20 million, or $3.3 million per year, through these programs. However, it has been forced to cut the aid to $3 million this past year because contributions have not kept up with increased costs. In fact, contributions have evidently dropped below previous years' levels. Slightly more than 2% of Chicago's parish revenues are redistributed in the form of subsidies to poorer parishes, and 20% of all parishes are involved in "twinning." But the diocese has printed no detailed records of redistributions through these programs. It appears that the Chicago archdiocese has been partially successful in its redistribution efforts.

Brooklyn has had limited success with a *required* form of twinning called clustering. The diocese assigns each parish to a cluster of three to five parishes. Parish leaders form a cluster board of pastors, laity, and school principals. Each cluster then assesses its own needs and decides which schools can be profitably combined or closed, and which resources can be shared most effectively. Clustering helps only in areas where *many* parishes need help. Wealthy parishes frequently observe only the formalities of clustering. Clustering has weakened parish bonds and, to that extent, may have damaged inner-city parishes. On the other hand, it did have marked success in a few inner-city areas.

Another diocesan approach to indirect subsidies is the assignment of an inner-city school to a church without a school or regular parishioners of its own, such as a church that serves downtown workers. Clearly this approach has only limited applicability, however, since there are few non-parish churches.

Subsidy programs increase the authority of the central school officials—superintendent and board—at some cost to the pastors and bishops. One of the greatest sources of conflict arises from the way central school officials must balance needs for their limited funds. Conflicts have risen to such intensity that bishops have been forced to overrule their school staff. The officials—often nuns, laity, and priests who have not risen in the hierarchy to the rank of pastor—require the pastor to submit a detailed accounting of his parish's revenues and expenses. Pastors are often reluctant to open their books to anyone other than their superiors, especially when the parish is in financial difficulties.

To avoid this problem, bishops sometimes bypass the board of education and help the pastor directly. The greatest objection to this personal approach is that it eliminates both the planning a parish must go through to prepare a budget statement and the careful review of proposals given by central school officials for each parish school.

3. **Community support:** In a number of cities, inner-city schools have turned to the surrounding community for help. Some schools remain attached to the diocesan system and simply appoint or elect boards of trustees from the business community. Other schools—either singly or in a group—separate themselves from the diocese and receive support from a public or community corporation. These schools do not change significantly from what they would have been if they had remained within the Catholic system. Their withdrawal simply facilitates their receiving aid.

The extreme variant of this approach has taken place in New York City, where the public school system has taken over private schools and kept the teaching staff. The arrangement has not proven satisfactory to the private schools, since their policies become enmeshed with the union and public schools system politics that plague inner-city public schools.

4. **Mission school financing:** There are two forms of this financing: (1) a religious order endowed to provide education to groups the school serves may raise funds for the school's educational efforts; (2) the school itself can mount a large direct-mail campaign asking for contributions. Of the two forms, the second is usually followed by schools with a more overtly public purpose that the public can more readily identify with, such as teaching American Indians.

5. **Public financing:** The Supreme Court has struck down state attempts to finance any portion of education provided directly by church-affiliated schools, although it has permitted state and federal governments to provide auxiliary and remedial services and some school supplies. No public programs can supply the basic educational costs of Catholic schools. There is no Constitutional prohibition on the direct and total support on unaffiliated private schools. In defense of First Amendment religious freedom, the Court has put the church in the ironic posi-

tion of having to abandon its inner-city schools in order to make them eligible for public funding. Existing programs applicable to Catholic inner-city schools do not help the schools pay their basic expenses, or prevent their financial collapse.

Conclusion

We have seen that the inner-city Catholic schools are different from most Catholic parish schools. They exist in economically declining areas where the population is becoming less dense, relatively poorer, and more minority. Their neighborhoods are particularly subject to rapid racial and ethnic changes. The parishes and schools cannot control any of these processes, and at best can attempt to adjust rapidly to them.

Their adjustment is made more difficult by the parochialism of the Catholic parish system, ironically also a great strength and virtue of the system. Racial and ethnic minorities enter parishes founded by previous ethnic residents. Because parishes form themselves so closely to the ethnic, cultural, economic and other characteristics of their parishioners, it is particularly difficult to incorporate newcomers with substantially different backgrounds and characteristics into the life of established parishes. Rapid changes in population will inevitably weaken once well-organized parishes.

The inner-city parishes could survive, in most cases, if the newcomers could be organized as effective parish members. This goal is problematic because recent newcomers are usually not Catholic or are traditionally inactive Catholics. Catholic parishes appear to have abandoned serious attempts to convert non-Catholics to the Catholic religion, perhaps in the spirit of Christian ecumenism. However, either inner-city parishes must revive this practice (when their neighborhoods are heavily non-Catholic), or they must enlist non-Catholics in active membership in Catholic parishes and in the active support and governance of Catholic schools. The third option, ignoring the non-Catholics, is certain to force the eventual collapse of parish and school. The active enlistment of non-Catholics in the affairs of Catholic parishes challenges the purposes of Catholic parishes and schools.

There are two primary means of supporting inner-city schools with large non-Catholic populations: central financing by the diocese or financing at the parish level. Diocesan financing will substantially change the relationship between the diocese and the wealthier parishes capable of underwriting the cost of inner-city schools—making diocesan decisions a matter of much greater local concern—and between the central authorities and the local parishes and schools receiving aid, giving central authorities far more control over local schools and consequently, making more difficult the task of recruiting local efforts to aid the school.

Parish financing in inner-city areas must rely on the contribution of work by parents and others on behalf of the school and the willingness of teachers, perhaps drawn from the parent pool, to forego part of their appropriate salaries. To obtain these contributions, the parish—or the school directly— must effectively organize parishioners and parents. A number of aspects of inner-city parishes make this organizing effort extremely difficult. The primary problem is that inner-city parishes have no time to build their weak community organizations into effective working bodies before having to face large financial crises.

Dioceses have attempted several solutions to these problems requiring the creation of new political forms through which the church can connect wealthier parishes to the inner-city and obtain from parishioners of the giving and receiving parishes alike, assent that central officials have the right to make decisions affecting both. Often the need for developing these new political relationships has been recognized too late, after important centrally designed programs have failed. Or diocesan officials recognize too late—after a school has closed—that substantial inner-city resources remained untapped for want of organization. Often church officials have substantially underestimated the public importance of inner-city schools, and have not understood until too late that non-Catholics in inner-city neighborhoods would fight to keep Catholic schools in their community.

Questions for Research

1. Although the parish is the basic organizational unit of the American Catholic church, there is surprisingly little written about how it operates. The literature of American civil government is replete with studies of town governments, community boards, community organizations and the like, which evaluate the mechanisms permitting citizens to take part in civil government, or examine the way the civil government is able to discover the needs of the community it serves. Inevitably, these studies discuss how new demands arise in the community and are expressed to those making decisions. Most studies include an analysis of the way public officials obtain support for their actions—how they organize and participate in political parties, meet informally with elites, or develop public charisma.

In the parish, the Catholic church has an astoundingly effective organizational unit—strong everywhere but in the inner city. Even in the inner city some strong parishes stand out. The leaders of the Catholic Church (and I include both clerics and laypersons in this group) must know much more about what makes parishes effective organizations. Parishes must be studied in the way local governments have been studied.

2. In recent years, dioceses have made a number of changes in their structures to develop greater lay and religious participation in the control of their schools. For the most part, these changes have been overlaid on existing, informal diocesan arrangements for directing school and parish projects, and little official recognition has been given to areas where the two approaches are incompatible. Serious conflicts have erupted in a number of dioceses, most notably in Chicago, which have damaged the relationships between the central authorities and the parish administrators, on the one hand, and lay and religious school leaders on the other. To understand how new institutions will affect a diocese, it is essential that the existing formal and informal structures of influence in the diocese be described. Dioceses must be studied to understand how new institutions will change them and what opposition can be expected from these changes.

3. The organizational success of the American Catholic Church has varied for different ethnic groups. Some are much more active participants in the organized church than others. For example, there are more Polish and Italian Catholics than there are Irish, but many more Irish religious and lay leaders. Is this pattern changing today? Are there institutional or organizational reasons why it has occurred? These questions are particularly important in an attempt to plan an effective strategy to organize the inner-city parishes into stronger units.

4. The church needs current data on the ethnic concentrations in inner-city schools. Are these schools disproportionately important to minorities? Would the closing of these schools in any large numbers have the effect of driving minorities out of the church? Are the schools particularly important to the steady increase in the number of black Catholics? Will minority membership and participation increase even without the schools?

Notes on Sources for Chapter 2

Joseph H. Fichter, *Parochial School—A Sociological Study* (Notre Dame, Indiana: University of Notre Dame Press, 1958)

Andrew Greeley, William McCready, and Kathleen McCourt, *Catholic Schools in a Declining Church* (Kansas City: Sheed and Ward, Inc., 1976)

Donald A. Erickson, Richard L. Nault and Bruce Cooper, assisted by Robert L. Lamborn, "Recent Enrollment Trends in the U.S. Nonpublic Schools," in Susan Abramowitz and Stuart Rosenfeld, editors, *Declining Enrollment: The Challenge of the Coming Decade* (Washington, D.C.: National Institute of Education, U.S. Government Printing Office, 1978)

Otto F. Kraushaar, *American Non-Public Schools: Patterns of Diversity.* (Baltimore and London: The Johns Hopkins University Press, 1972)

James Michael Lee, editor, "Catholic Education in the United States," *Catholic Education in the Western World* (Notre Dame, Indiana: University of Notre Dame Press, 1967) pp. 253-312.

Reginald A. Neuwein, editor, *Catholic Schools in Action: A Study of Catholic Elementary and Secondary Schools in the U.S.* (Notre Dame and London: University of Notre Dame Press, 1966)

James Sanders, "The Education of Chicago Catholics: An Urban History" (unpublished Ph.D. dissertation, Department of History, University of Chicago, 1970)

Thomas Vitullo-Martin and Julia Vitullo-Martin, "The Politics of Alternative Models to the Public Schools," U.S. Office of Education grant No. OEC-9-720013 (057), (ERIC, 1973)

Thomas Vitullo-Martin with the assistance of Julia Vitullo-Martin and Glenn Pasanen, "Parents, Policies and Political Structures: A Study of Policies and Parental Support in Catholic Schools," National Institute of Education grant No. NE-G-00-3-0150, forthcoming.

In addition, worthwhile discussions of the finance and politics of Catholic schools are found in:

Ernest Bartel, *Costs and Benefits of Catholic Elementary and Secondary Schools* (Notre Dame, Indiana: University of Notre Dame Press, 1969)

Donald Erickson, *Crisis in Illinois Nonpublic Schools,* Research Report to the Elementary and Secondary Schools Study Commission, State of Illinois, 1971.

Donald Erickson and John Donovan (with the assistance of George F. Madaus, George Lundy and Associates), *The Three R's of NonPublic Education in Louisiana: Race, Religion, and Region,* A Report to the President's Commission on School Finance (OEC-0-72-0339), January, 1972.

Frank J. Fahey, editor, *Economic Problems of Non-Public Schools*, A Report to the President's Commission on School Finance (Notre Dame, Indiana: University Office of Educational Research, 1971)

Louis R. Gary, et al., *The Collapse of Nonpublic Education: Rumor or Reality?* The Report on Nonpublic Education in the State of New York for the New York State Commission on the Quality, Cost and Financing of Elementary and Secondary Education, 2 vols., (New York: Implication Research, Inc., 1971)

National Catholic Education Association, *National Conference on Catholic School Finance, 1975* (Washington, D.C.: NCEA, 1975)

National Catholic Reporter, and various archdiocesan newspapers.

John F. O'Leary, Jr.; David A. Tierno; and John T. Gurash, Chairman, The Report of the Archdiocesan Advisory Committee on the Financial Crisis of Catholic Schools in Philadelphia and Surrounding Counties, (Philadelphia: Archdiocese of Philadelphia, 1972)

University of Michigan, School of Education, *The Financial Implications of Changing Patterns of Non-public School Operations in Chicago, Detroit, Milwaukee, and Philadelphia,* A Report to the President's Commission on School Finance (Ann Arbor, 1971)

CHAPTER 3

PUBLIC PURPOSES OF CATHOLIC SCHOOLS

The crux of the inner-city school problem is not "Can the church support the schools?" but "Why should it?" If the church has reasons to support tne schools, it has tne ability. Some would argue that the schools provide more benerits to the public than to the church, so the government should help support tnem. And if the government retuses, then the schools should close.

There is a flaw in this reasoning. First, the church's interest in supporting the schools ought not to be tied to the government's willingness to act. Either tne schools are a responsibility of Catholics, or they are not. If the schools are, Catholics may have an easier time of it with government help, but they are capable of going it alone. If the schools are not, then there is no reason for Catnolics to join the government in aiding the schools.

Ultimately any discussion of preserving and expanding Catholic schools must face the question of what good the schools do the church. This chapter will discuss some of the principal public benefits of inner-city Catholic schools. I am arguing that inner-city schools have different benefits from traditional Catholic schools, which typically serve parishioners. For one reason or another, many inner-city schools serve non-parishioners. Should the church restrict its efforts to preserve schools with viable parishes? Should it use the schools as a base for building up new parishes in the inner-city? Should it provide schools to serve the non-Catholic community or the public, thereby cutting the schools' ties with parishes?

I will not review here the church's need for Catholic schools to educate Catholic children. The consideration of aid to inner-city schools assumes agreement on the importance of Catholic education systems. In addition, inner-city schools serve the church in a special way. First, in serving the residents of the inner-city, the church will earn respect among the lower-income people who live there and will increase its own self-respect by mitigating the effects of an historical accident which has left the American Catholic Church a 98% white church in a country that is over 11% black. Second, the principal public benefits of Catholic schools—strengthening families, improving inner-city neighborhoods, and improving opportunities for minorities through higher-quality education—are matters of concern to the church and should not be left to the government alone.

Effect of Private Schools on Public Schools

Much of the opposition to aiding inner-city Catholic schools, among Catholic and public leaders responsible for formulating public policy, hinges on the belief that Catholic schools hinder the attainment of the democratic goals of public education: They provide a solution for those who, if they were forced to enroll their children in public schools, would attend to the problems of those schools. Some of these persons say Catholic schools are racist havens, and even if they are not deliberately racist, they exacerbate the problems of integrating public schools. The position was unwittingly well-expressed by an important academic policy analyst at a recent meeting of graduate school professors and high public officials who were discussing New York City's crisis. The professor suggested the major problems of the city's public schools—public support, bureaucratic reform, and racial integration—would be solved in a stroke if the city simply closed its private schools. His view was not challenged, despite the contradictions inherent in his position.

• **Public support:** Certainly the New York experience does not support the thesis that public schools fail to obtain needed support because large percentages of parents use private schools to educate their children. More than 25% of the city's elementary and secondary students attend private schools. And more private school family heads are likely to be voters, given their demographic characteristics, so the influence of the 25% on public officials should be disproportionately strong. The presence of this private school population has not adversely affected the level of financial support for public education in New York City. The city spends $3,400 per pupil on public education, more than any other major American city. In the elementary grades, the city spends more per pupil than all but a handful of the most expensive private schools and more than five times the per-pupil expenditure of the average Catholic inner-city school.

The evidence against this thesis is even more dramatic than present expenditure levels suggest. New York City has increased its per-pupil spending in the public schools by an incredible 300% in the past eight years. Just what were the damaging effects of the large private school population? The city system, in fact, makes money on its private school students. The state allocates, but does not deliver, $300 in services for every child in private school. The enormous increase in expenditure has produced no measurable increase in basic education. Instead, the number of average class hours of instruction per pupil has dropped, and average pupil achievent has declined. The record suggests that increasing the support levels does not measurably correct the school's basic problems. Given this record, it is misguided to call for the sacrifice of the private schools to increase support for the public schools. Support would not increase. Rather, as I will argue, the closing of private schools is likely to decrease support for the public.

• **Bureaucratic reform:** Similarly, it is unrealistic to believe increasing the public schools' monopoly in education would bring about any improvements in its bureaucracy. In other areas of city services, this is recognized. No one seriously argues, for example, that New York City would be cleaner if it closed all the private cartage firms and left all refuse to the Department of Sanitation. Or, that city parks would improve if it closed all the private parks, such as the Bronx Zoo, the Botanical Gardens, Gramercy Park, and so on.

• **Racial integration:** The effects of private schools on racial integration require a more developed argument. It is only sensible to attempt to discover the major forces encouraging the segregation of urban schools, and then look at the effect of private schools on those forces, rather than—as the academics did—simply presume that because private schools are present in cities, and enroll smaller proportions of minority students (as in some cases they do), they are thereby segregating the cities. In essence, the position rests on the assumption that by providing a choice, the private school hinders the public school's achievement of socially desirable goals. The concern is not the private school's *intention, policies, or even its racial characteristics* (the question of whether it is integrated is not asked), but the *effects* of its presence on the public school. "If private schools were closed, there would be enough whites to integrate meaningfully the public schools of our city" is a frequently heard comment.

If we reformulate the position, a flaw in its reasoning becomes clear: private schools allow people to escape unpopular, but socially desirable, situations in the public schools. Parents can thus frustrate public school authorities' attempts to balance the racial composition of their schools. Consequently, if the private schools are closed, parents are deprived of their ability to escape the public school integration policies. This conclusion is logical only if parents have no other way of avoiding public school integration policies (policies, we should note, which parents may find objectionable for reasons having nothing to do with racial attitudes).

52

In the thesis that "closing private schools would increase integration in the public," there are several unexamined assumptions. First, the position assumes the private schools in the vicinity of the racially impacted public schools are not integrated, and that parents are switching to private schools to escape minorities in the public schools. It would hardly make sense to move the children into schools with minorities. Unfortunately for the position, there are a surprisingly large number of minorities in private schools. In the West, there is a greater proportion of private school minority students. Proportionately more blacks are enrolled in private elementary schools than whites (i.e., 7% of blacks, 6% of whites). Minority enrollments are particularly important in certain diocese: In Mobile and in Birmingham dioceses (Alabama), 32% and 43% respectively of all Catholic school students are blacks. In the Catholic schools in the District of Columbia, 77% of the elementary and 50% of the high school students are minorities. In the diocese of New York, approximately 50% of the elementary students are Spanish-surnamed or other minorities. Minorities are an increasing portion of Catholic students.

What happens to the argument if the private schools are more integrated, or educate proportionately more minorities than the public? Then, to close private schools fosters racial *segregation.*

This is exactly what happened when Catholic and other private schools in the South were segregated by the Black Codes, laws affirmed by the Supreme Court in the 1917 *Berea College Case.* After the 1954 *Brown* decision struck down the school segregation statutes, private schools were the first to integrate voluntarily. In St. Louis, New Orleans, and elsewhere, Catholic schools integrated *before* the public systems. In Mobile, Birmingham, and other southern cities, whites fled to the segregated public system to avoid integration in Catholic schools. The effect of integrated Catholic schools was to break the back of resistance to voluntary desegregation in the public systems of those cities. When the laws required segregation, the private schools were the last hold-outs against it. When the segregationist laws were struck down, they were the first to integrate on their own initiative. Hence, the reasoning rests on factual assumptions about private schools which are erroneous.

Second, the reasoning has turned the policy objectives inside out. Integrationists focus on the integration of public schools for the sake of fostering an integrated community, but our academics have assumed an identity between the objectives of the school integration policies and the goal of integrating the community, an identity which does not exist. What constitutes an "integrated public" school is defined by a number of arbitrary local rules. Public schools are considered integrated, for example, when their average minority population approaches the minority percentage in their jurisdiction. After that point is reached, the schools are under no further legal compulsion to integrate. Accidentally or legally, public school jurisdictions are racially gerrymandered, so public schools can be integrated in the eyes of the law even when they are predominantly minority, if the population they serve—their jurisdiction—is predominantly minority. In fact, an integration policy which sparks a white exodus can effectively foster public school integration, not because it improves racial balances in the schools, but because it hurts the balances in the community.

In the first three years of Court-mandated integration of Boston's public schools, the system lost 50,000 white students, almost half its white student population. The minority proportion of the public schools increased dramatically, but because most of these white students went to schools outside the city, the public schools actually became more integrated in a technical sense. The city itself became more segregated. Public school officials responsible for integration have technical school integration as their first objective; they are not responsible for integrating the city itself or for fostering integration in any other private or public organization in the city.

A particularly striking example of this attitude occurred recently in New York. A public elementary and intermediate school proposed a $1,000,000 Emergency School Assistance Act (ESAA) grant-request to the federal government. The school claimed the money would foster integration by attracting white students from private schools in the community. It argued that the community had enough white students to integrate the public school, but these students were enrolled in private schools. To attract the white student transferees, the public school proposed to establish programs and electives superior to those offered by the private schools.

The public school planners ignored the fact that the private schools in the community were all effectively integrated. The most reasonable expectation would be that the grant would attract minorities to the public schools, since the cost of private school tuitions, even with substantial grants and aid, is more difficult for lower-income families to bear. The most likely result of the massive federal expenditure would be to segregate further the public and the private schools simultaneously, by inducing minorities to leave the private schools.

If the project were successful in attracting a large number of whites as well, the likely effect would have been to make it more difficult for the private schools to offer scholarships to minorities and would, perhaps, have forced those schools to close. A marginal gain for integration in public schools—at great cost—would threaten integration in private schools.

Third, the reasoning assumes that competition from private schools is producing the racial isolation in the public, as if the private schools have drawn all the white children. Private school populations were greater before the period of "white flight." Today they enroll only slightly fewer minorities than the public. The choice they offer is not sufficient explanation for the level of *de facto* segregation developing around our major cities. The reasoning failed to consider the possibility that there were other alternatives draining whites from the city. The analysis is like attempting to control automobile exhaust pollution by closing AMC, and not touching GM.

How Parent Choice Affects Schools and Cities

It is obvious that parents choose private schools for their children. Precisely the same is true for most parents sending their children to public schools. Parents normally choose among public schools and their systems by moving. They pay a kind of entrance fee for their newly chosen public school in the purchase price or rent of their house. If all other amenities are equal, a home in a desirable school district is worth far more than one in a school district with a poor academic reputation. (Homeowners thus recover their entrance fee to the public schools, as long as the quality of the schools in the district does not disintegrate. Renters, since they are not building equity in their property, do not recover the increased level of rent.) In addition, parents using public schools pay a kind of tuition in the form of taxes which support the school. In the wealthiest districts and in specialized suburban districts where schools comprise virtually the only governmental service and where only families of school-aged children move, the connection between the tax tuition is quite clear. It is more hidden elsewhere, but just as real.

In sum, mostly all public and private schools are chosen by parents, and therefore compete with one another to attract parent-clients. Private schools which allow their quality to drop, or fail to supply parents with what they want, simply close. Public schools, on the other hand, cannot fail because of incompetence or even open hostility to their students. Public schools can muddle on, or move into another school attendance area. Few public school principals or superintendents would accept such a state, and so public schools also normally compete to attract families as clients.

The schools compete to induce parents and students to choose them. Not all schools can be chosen with equal ease, however. Some can be chosen only by a family's changing residence; others by competitive application (as are required by some specialized high schools such as Brona High School of science); others by paying tuition. Individuals vary in their ability to move their homes—especially into the most desirable school districts —or to pay tuition. All schools are in competition, but the competition is biased, with options open to some families, but not to others. Ironically, the most exclusive schools, the ones least accessible to most people, are public schools. The entrance requirement into the best public schools in the best public districts is the ability to purchase a very expensive home.

Types of Public School/Private School Competition

Let us examine the competition affecting these schools more closely, from the point of view of policy-analysts attempting to discover what policies will most improve the quality of education available to minorities, and will most advance the integration of the community. In choosing schools, we see two relevant types of competition: micro-competition, which occurs principally among the schools within a defined neighborhood or community; and macro-competition, which occurs among schools in different localities, sometimes within the same system but most often in different systems.

Micro-competition: Micro-competition takes place between schools attempting to attract students living in the same neighborhood. Typically, the competition is between a public school and one or more private schools. Because neighborhoods are generally comprised of residents whose incomes and social status are similar, the micro-competition between the public and private schools tends not to divide the community along class lines. We even find, in the more solidly ethnic neighborhoods, little difference in the religious affiliation of the public and private school students. Both public and private schools, with some minor differences, resemble their neighborhood's socioeconomic characteristics. In this case, competitions tend to occur over the substance of the school's curricula or pedagogical approach.

Because families do not have to move to enroll a child in the private school, competition between public and private schools tends not to encourage racial and economic segregation of the community. Private schools often help stabilize neighborhoods by providing parents, who are considering public schools elsewhere, with an alternative that permits them to stay in the neighborhood.

Macro-competition: Macro-competition takes place between schools in different neighborhoods, predominantly in public schools where students are assigned on the basis of residence. Families continue to choose schools, but in order to choose, they must relocate. Hence, public schools compete by attracting new residents to their attendance area. School competition is reflected in housing cost. The more desirable the schools, the higher the housing rent or selling price (all other housing characteristics being equal). Housing costs are far more effective than private school tuitions in blocking the admission of low-income families. The competition among public schools encourages residential segregation along economic class lines.

When urban private schools offer education equal with the best suburban public schools, they help stem the flight of the middle and upper-middle class families who normally find homes in prestigious suburbs. The opposite is also true. Inner-city Catholic schools help to keep inner-city families who have begun to move up the economic ladder and who would—if there were no Catholic schools present—move out to a more distant part of the city or inner-ring suburb where the schools have a good reputation.

The attraction of the inner-city Catholic school for the most successful inner-city families is an important aspect of the schools' contribution to the inner-city.

Private schools aid public schools by helping to keep families (with the means to move out) in the city. First, they help increase the tax base, to which public school revenues are keyed. (The greater the demand for housing, the more a house is worth, the greater the revenues from property taxes, the more income for the public schools.) Second, they help increase public school income derived from local sales and income taxes. The more families with higher incomes in an area, the more demand for goods and services and therefore the more sales and income tax revenues for the public schools. Third, the private school helps build political support for the public school, by helping keep more families with a stake in the neighborhood from moving away.

Residents of a neighborhood, especially property owners, tend to support and build public institutions which serve it, especially public schools because they so strongly influence housing values. Thus neighborhood public schools tend to receive increased political support because of the presence of private schools. Certainly parents who live in the city and send their children to private schools are more concerned and active in supporting the *city's* public schools than are parents who have moved to the suburbs and have become active in suburban political life.

Public schools which draw parents from the city to the suburbs hurt private schools as much—perhaps more—than they do the city's public schools. For example, private schools in New York have been financially damaged by the middle-class exodus partially caused by the decline of the New York City public schools in the face of stiff suburban school competition. As the number of middle-class families with school-aged children dwindles, fewer are left to choose city private schools.

Suburban public schools, with their enormous tax advantages, spend more than even the best city private schools—at a fraction of the cost to the parents. Wealthy parents, who may be liable for as much as 70% of their earned income for federal, state and local income taxes, must pay private school tuitions *in after-tax dollars* (thus more than trippling the portion of gross income which must be spent on the school tuition). For example, when income is taxed at 70%, one must earn $10,000 to pay a $3,000 tuition. However, those same parents pay property taxes —which are the principal support of public schools—in before-tax dollars so $3,000 of tax liability consumes only $3,000 of gross income. (In fact, if that $3,000 were spent on non-deductible expenses, it would become less than $1,000 after-tax dollars.)

The Central City Viewpoint

From the city's viewpoint, it is important that there be schools of perceived superior quality. Such schools raise the level of satisfaction of parents with continued residence in the area and increase neighborhood economic and social stability. The schools of superior quality in a neighborhood help the area compete against superior schools elsewhere—in other neighborhoods and in other systems.

Private schools are an important source of superior quality education, and therefore act as conservative forces resisting both the predatory pressures of the suburban systems on the central cities and the racial and class segregation of cities fostered by the organizational pattern of public schools.

The greatest damage to urban public schools, and to the character of the cities themselves, comes from *macro*-, not *micro*-, competitions: the most powerful competitors against urban public schools, which spend more per child than either public or private schools in the central city can afford.

Private schools are not the enemy of public schools. Urban public school spokespersons view private schools as the enemy because they ignore the macro-competition and see only the micro-competition. They prefer to see suburban public schools as irresponsible. If they set their attention on the welfare of the city itself, however, and agreed that any school which educates children well, keeps families in the city, and maintains neighborhood stability is a school to be supported, their position on such public policy proposals as the recent tuition tax credit plan would very likely change.

Private schools in central cities help those areas resist the *predations* of the suburban public schools. To the extent they succeed, they stabilize their neighborhoods and aid the public schools. Even in the most simplistic analysis, it is to the advantage of the city to have wealthy residents whose children attend private schools because their presence directly raises city tax revenues and indirectly increases them again through demand effects on the local economy and multiplier effects. A sophisticated analysis would show substantial advantages to the arrangement for public schools.

Private School Integration Effects: Summary

The macro-competition between public and private schools is extremely damaging to the social goals of many education reformers (such as integration and assimilation of ethnics) because the intra-regional competition encourages economic segregation. To the extent that the competition cuts urban schools' tax base and deprives them of their most politically sophisticated supporters, the competition damages them directly. As the city is damaged, the private schools concentrated there are also damaged.

The micro-competition between private and public schools serving the same neighborhoods achieves goals often pursued by reformers. Especially in the inner-city, the micro-competition tends to take place over the perceived quality of academic programs offered by the various schools. By winning—and inner-city private schools, despite inferior resources, record significantly superior academic achievements on the average—private schools set standards that public schools must reach. The competition improves the quality of public education.

Inner-city School Benefits: Education

In the first section of this chapter, we discussed the way the *choices* presented by private inner-city schools (and other urban private schools) can aid the city and its public schools. Our discussion concentrated on the indirect benefits of the schools. In the remaining portion of this chapter, we will discuss the literature which assesses the direct benefits of the schools: How good are the schools? How well do they teach language and mathematical skills? Do they provide an exceptional or an average base for further academic progress in college? Are they socially divisive? Do they teach students values that hinder the social integration of the nation's many immigrant groups?

In each of these areas there is an implied comparison: is the performance of private schools better, worse, or in any way different from that of public schools?

The literature on parochial inner-city schools is extremely small and too overly specialized to consider in isolation from the broader literature discussing the characteristics and effects of private schools. In our discussion, we will review the literature that attempts to assess what the effects of Catholic schools are and what Catholic schools do to produce them. In reviewing the literature, we must be extremely cautious to avoid conclusions which *assume* that private schools are necessarily responsible for the superior results of their students in achievement tests— in other words, that private schools are measurably better in a given area because they have a superior educational practice. The key word is "assume." Private schools may have superior programs, or better teachers, and these may explain the superior performance of their students. But it may be that the schools select only the better students, or expel the most difficult ones. Or they may be located in neighborhoods which are economically well-off, making comparisons with heavier-lower-income enrollments in public schools invalid. With sufficient care, good comparisons can be made, but analysts have too infrequently taken sufficient care.

Teaching Catholicism

The classic study of the effects of Catholic education is

Andrew Greeley and Peter Rossi's *The Education of Catholic Americans* (1966). The authors asked, "Do Catholics educated in Catholic schools make better Catholics?" They found Catholic schools, taken as a whole, only moderately successful in making their students better Catholics. Students from actively religious families emerge from Catholic schools more conscientious Catholics, but students from religious families who do not attend Catholic schools differ little from their Catholic school counterparts in belief or behavior. Students from moderately religious or non-religious Catholic families are only minimally influenced by Catholic schooling.

However, inner-city Catholic schools enrolling substantial numbers of non-Catholics were not as evident 15 years ago when the Greeley-Rossi study was conducted. Their study was based on a national sample that could not single out the experience in inner-city schools. There has been no broad study of the effect of inner-city Catholic schools on the beliefs and behavior of the students who have attended them. Observers in Detroit and Chicago have noted that the schools do have an effect on Catholic membership and on the vitality of inner-city parishes. Chicago's Holy Angels parish claims the largest Catholic instruction classes and the highest number of new converts of any parish in the country (80 in 1976), and attributes its success to the presence of the school. The school enables the parish to extend itself into the non-Catholic community. The school's quality, its reputation for discipline, and its emphasis on moral strength and individual responsibility have built a reputation for the parish which has encouraged community residents to join the church. Other converts are the result of active parish efforts. The parish requires all children, Catholic and non-Catholic, to receive religious instruction. All students are expected to attend some church service each week. Children who belong to other parishes or non-Catholic churches are expected to attend their own services. The parish receives reports on attendance from the pastors and ministers of the parishes or churches. The school requires all non-Catholic parents to take religious instruction, which parallels the instruction their children receive in the school. The school and parish take the position that the children's education is the parents' responsibility, and that it would be irresponsible for the parents to commit their children to instruction in a religion they know nothing about. Observers in Detroit have also noted that the most stable inner-city parishes have schools.

In sum, researchers have found little behavior effect of Catholic education that is independent of the family's own religious practices. This is either an indication that the schools have little effect on future behavior, or that their effects were not discovered by the researchers' questions. In either case, existing research has not considered more recent examples of inner-city Catholic schools. We therefore know little about how the inner-city schools do, or do not, further the growth of Catholic beliefs and practices. Scattered observers have noted that the schools have some organizational effects on inner-city parishes, increasing church visibility and membership and helping support the parish. Greeley, McCready and McCourt emphasized this role of Catholic schools in their more recent book, *Catholic Schools in a Declining Church (1977)*.

Basic quality education: It has long been feared by Catholic school proponents, and argued by their critics, that the unusually poorly equipped Catholic schools impede the success of their students. Catholic schools rarely have such educational niceties as laboratories, audiovisual aids, library books, special programs, etc. Their classrooms are frequently overcrowded, and their teachers have less training and fewer advanced degrees than public school teachers. (While qualifications of the teaching sisters have increased continually for the past 20 years, their numbers have declined dramatically. Parish schools have, in general, been unable to compete with public schools for lay teachers with the best training and most advanced degrees). The disadvantage of the Catholic schools is particularly pronounced in the inner-city and is reflected in inner-city per pupil expenditures. Observers estimate public schools spend three to eight times the amount spent per pupil in inner-city Catholic schools, the variations reflecting differences in public school expenditure from one system to another, rather than significant differences in Catholic inner-city school spending. For example, Philadelphia reports public school expenditures of about $1,700 vs. New York's approximately $3,400 per pupil. Inner-city Catholic schools in both cities spend $500 to $750. It is therefore reasonable to believe that Catholic school children would be less successful because of these disadvantages. Are they?

Greeley and Rossi's surprising answer is no. Catholic school children not only do not underachieve, they overachieve. It is normal in the United States for children to reach a higher level of education than their parents, but not usually a whole level higher. Children of parents who did not finish grade school, for example, are unlikely to finish college. But poorer Catholics pursue their education further in Catholic schools than do similar Catholics and non-Catholics in public schools. While non-Catholic school students finish high school, similar Catholic students are more likely to complete college.

Greeley and Rossi's study was particularly important because it used a more meaningful test of the impact of the school on the students than is normally employed, and because of its superior research methodology. Newspapers commonly print comparisons of the performance of public school students and Catholics on standardized achievement tests, and these comparisons are regularly and properly dismissed by informed readers as invalid. Student achievement is heavily influenced by the socioeconomic status of their family. Unless an analyst has carefully selected a study-group (or sample) from the public schools that matches the socioeconomic characteristics of another selected from the Catholic, comparisons between the two groups are invalid. Put quite simply, when we read the newspaper comparison, we do not know if Catholic schools are better because they do a more effective job of teaching, or because they do not have as many children from lower socioeconomic status families. Greeley and Rossi compared the results of Catholic and public schooling on a carefully matched sample of Catholics who had used Catholic schools, Catholics who used public schools, and non-Catholics who used public schools. They found the Catholic schools more effective, but only for children from lower-income families who would not be expected to do well in public schools.

Gregory Hancock, of the University of Chicago, found a similar pattern in a controlled study of private and public schools in Chicago. Hancock selected Catholic and public schools serving similar students at upper, middle and lower-income levels. Using academic achievement as a measure of academic success, Hancock found that lower-income children in Catholic schools achieve at faster rates than similar children in public schools. By comparing schools serving the same neighborhoods, Hancock substantially neutralized differences in socioeconomic background as a factor confounding comparison between public and private. In fact, he found that Catholic school students in his sample schools had lower median I.Q.'s than the public school students. Since I.Q. is also related to socioeconomic status, this observation tended to confirm the fact that he was dealing with comparable student populations. Catholic schools in the lower and lower-middle income neighborhoods attained substantially the same median reading level at grade three as the public, and substantially higher levels by grade six. The advantage rested with Catholic schools despite significantly lower per-pupil expenditures and higher pupil-teacher ratios. In the lower-income black neighborhoods, the advantage of the Catholic schools was most pronounced: by grade six, their students' median achievement was six to nine months ahead of the companion public school students. However, Hancock also observes that upper-middle-income children achieve higher median levels in public schools than their counterparts in Catholic schools.

Neither Greeley and Rossi nor Hancock explains *why* the lower-income Catholic school students outperform their public school counterparts.

A group of Rhode Island researchers, headed by David Morton of the University of Rhode Island (Ewing, Brittingham, and Morton) has studied the literature in an attempt to explain the differences between Rhode Island Public and Catholic school students' achievement on standardized tests. They found:

1. There are significant differences between Iowa Test of Basic Skills (ITBS) achievement test score distributions of public and parochial (almost all Catholic) school students in Rhode Island; the differences are greater at the eighth grade than at the fourth.

2. In general, differences in ITBS score distributions based on national norms occur at the middle and lower end of the distribution. No substantial differences in achievement between public and parochial school students are found among those scoring at the top of their respective distributions. (This would suggest that equally proportionate numbers of public and private school students would win competitive academic awards, presuming proportionate applications.)

3. Differences in achievement between public and parochial school students are greatest in language and least in mathematics.

Their most surprising finding was that the distance between parochial and public school achievement was increasing in favor of parochial schools for the past decade, both in Rhode Island and nationally. The reason was not that parochial schools improved their scores, but rather that public school scores declined. Why, they asked, did the parochial schools hold firm while public schools' achievement levels dropped?

Explaining Parochial School Superiority

In searching the literature, the Rhode Island researchers found more difficulties than possible explanations. They found that "school policy, curriculum and instructional method, and student socioeconomic background and motivation were variables frequently identified as potential causes of the differences in achievement." But they also found in the literature that individual public and private schools differed substantially on these items: "Studies of public and parochial school curriculum confirmed a general similarity between them." Individual schools may have a differential impact on student achievement, but the circumstances producing the effect were not consistent for all public or private schools. The comparison of public to parochial was therefore a doubtful project, since the two did not constitute discrete categories of schools with substantial numbers of shared characteristics.

The Rhode Island group reviewed the literature for evidence about the character of private school students or their schools that could explain the relative success of the schools. They found that higher private school scores were not explained by the higher socioeconomic background of the students, because private and public school students had similar backgrounds. According to a study by Brickell, Rhode Island parochial school family incomes were $7,000 in 1966, which was average for the state. The Rhode Island group also found that, measured by the Blau-Duncan Occupational Prestige Index, Rhode Island Catholic families were on a par with Protestant families, so possible Catholic superiority in the education of the head of the household was ruled out.

A recent study by the Bureau of the Census (1976 Survey of Income and Education) supported this conclusion for the national parochial school population. The bureau's survey found that 6% of all students whose family incomes were under $1,000* were enrolled in private schools, and that 7% of all with family incomes at the $7,500 poverty level, or below, were in private schools. This figure is surprisingly high, since private schools enroll only 9% of all students nationally and only a slightly smaller proportion of children from the lowest-income families. The percentages for *parochial* schools would be even higher because most low-income students in private schools are in parochial schools. Finally, the percentages of low-income students would be higher still at the parochial *elementary* level because tuitions and admissions tests at the secondary level tend to screen out some of the students from the lowest-income families. Differences in socioeconomic character of the two groups

---

* The Bureau of Census counts only cash income in its tabulation of family income. Hence, in states where Public Assistance payments are made "in-kind," as in the form of subsidized housing or direct payment of rent to the landlord, families can live with extremely low amounts of income. All dollars are 1975 dollars.

are unlikely to explain the general superiority of the parochial schools.

The Morton group found that selection by the schools could not explain the parochial school's superior performance. They cited Lee, who found parish and diocesan schools to have near open admissions at the elementary level, and more selective (usually academically competitive) admissions at the secondary level. Brickell found that "the average IQ of parochial elementary school students was 105 versus 103 for the public school students." However, he found the average I.Q. at Catholic secondary schools to be 120 in Rhode Island, indicating the effects of selectivity in those schools. Selectivity at the elementary level does not explain superior Catholic school performance.

Although the school may not be selective, the parents most interested in quality education may select parochial schools—there may be a self-selection. No doubt faced with a specific choice between a public and a parochial school, some parents will decide the parochial school is superior. If there is a consensus among parents that parochial schools are superior, we must return to our original question. Why would parents make that choice? In the inner-city in particular, why would parents pay tuition to schools that are overcrowded, understaffed, undersupplied, and spend only a fraction of what the public schools spend per pupil? The private schools are not the obvious choice for parents pursuing the best interests of their children, if parents judge by school resources. Furthermore, a substantial portion of parents must select parochial schools out of a concern for religious education. There is no reason to believe the children of these parents should be academically more able, sufficient to explain the superior performance of their schools in achievement tests.

Another possible explanation for private school superiority is that they might expel or refuse to re-admit enough low-achieving students to raise their achievement. The excluded students would then enroll in public schools, bringing down public school averages. No researcher has found any extensive use of expulsion sufficient to explain the statistical differences in achievement rates of the two sets of schools. The most careful study has been dont by Nault, of the Saint Louis-area private secondary schools (reported on Table 1). He found that 30% of the schools in his sample failed to exercise their power to expel, terminate, or otherwise exclude students from enrolling in the school. He found that parochial secondary schools excluded an average of only 2.2 students per year (average school population was 532), too few to have an discernible affect on achievement averages, even if excluded students were uniformly low achievers. Catholic high schools reserve expulsion for relatively serious offenses, such as drug abuse and stealing. In the elementary schools, there are fewer instances of these offenses and, in recent years, a tendency to deal with problem students rather than dismiss them. In a survey of 47 schools, the expulsion or other exclusion of students from parochial elementary schools was rare.

Table 1

AVERAGE PERCENTAGES OF STUDENTS
EXPELLED, TERMINATED AND EXCLUDED DURING THE 1974-75
ACADEMIC YEAR IN SURVEYED NON-PUBLIC SECONDARY
SCHOOLS, REPORTED BY SCHOOL TYPES

School Type	Average Percentage of Students Expelled	Average Percentage of Students Terminated	Average Percentage of Students Excluded
Roman Catholic Parish of Diocese	0.53% (N = 25)	0.74% (N = 8)	1.53% (N = 25)
Roman Catholic Order[1]	0.57% (N = 20)	1.73% (N = 16)	1.97% (N = 20)
Other Sectarian	2.1% (N = 4)	1.85% (N = 4)	3.96% (N = 4)
Independent	1.73% (N = 9)	2.51% (N = 7)	3.67% (N = 9)
ALL SCHOOLS	0.84% (N = 58)	1.67% (N = 35)	1.85% (N = 58)

[1] Schools maintained by Roman Catholic religious communities, from Nault (1976), p. 21. Table 7.

The Rhode Island team found that Brickell offered a useful explanation of the superiority of Catholic schools in Rhode Island:

"Although the subjects taught in public and parochial schools were the same, the amount of time spent on them differed. Parochial schools spent one-half of each school day on language arts development at the intermediate level. And because religion class was added to the parochial school day after state requirements had been met, the parochial school student was exposed to 150 minutes of instruction per week more than the public. Although the subject was religion, the students still employed language arts skills. At the elementary level, this may have import in light of Carroll's time-needed-for learning/ time-spent-in-learning theory. The time needed by a student to learn a specific task or achieve a goal is influenced by his/her ability to understand instruction, his/her aptitude, and by the quality of the instruction. The time allotted for learning and the perseverance of the student are determined by the time a student actually spends in learning."

In their own investigations of conditions in parochial and public schools that might explain the superiority of the parochial schools serving lower-income students, the Rhode Island group found that teacher attitudes toward their students, their feeling of efficacy, expectations of success and job satisfaction were similar in upper and middle socioeconomic status public and parochial schools, and in lower-status parochial schools. Teacher attitude changed markedly for the worse in lower-status public schools. The group could make no argument about whether teacher attitude caused the superior performance in the lower-status parochial schools and the decline in the public, or if the respective success or failure of the schools determined the teachers' attitudes.*

In this review, certain features stand out. Lower-income parochial schools are particularly successful when compared to public schools serving the same socioeconomic groups. Middle and upper-income Catholic schools perform comparably to public schools, with some fall-off in Catholic school performance at upper socioeconomic levels. Comparative studies show in-school attitudes in lower socioeconomic parochial schools to be most similar to those in middle and upper parochial and public schools. Inner-city schools fall into the lower-socioeconomic group. What is different about inner-city parochial schools that makes them more successful than comparable public schools?

Benefits of inner-city schools to families and neighborhoods: The impact of schools on families has not been studied. More attention has been paid to the impact of the family on student achievements, but much of this discussion has focused on characteristics beyond the family's control, such as its socioeconomic status, primary language spoken at home, or its behavioral pathologies. Two studies of Catholic schools conducted for the Office of Education and the National Institute of Education, indicated that Catholic schools—especially Catholic inner-city

---

* Appendix A presents a summation of the Rhode Island team's original research comparing public and parochial achievement rates

schools—were remarkably effective in obtaining the personal involvement of parents. This and other research reviewed by Morton suggests that this parental involvement may be responsible for the superior achievement of students. Catholic inner-city schools obtain this involvement because they are projects of their parishes: they belong to, are formed and sustained by, and serve the local Catholic community. Lower-income Catholics in inner-city Catholic schools are typically first or second-generation ethnics or recent migrants from rural areas. With the parish, the Catholic schools typically celebrate the rituals and events of the ethnic community. For instance, a Mexican-American Catholic school celebrated Mexican national and religious holidays as well as parish feasts, such as the patron saint's name day. We found these parish schools to be highly integrated into the family and communal life of the neighborhood. In this, they distinguished themselves from the public schools, which were usually staffed by teachers who were foreign to the neighborhood's culture and who normally lived elsewhere. The religious life of an ethnic family and community is an important cohesive force helping to create a sense of unity among its members.

The public school must transform a religious celebration into something secular and objectivized to observe ethnic feasts, or it will celebrate only American holidays. For these and other reasons, the public school weakens the bases of family and social cohesion in the ethnic community. From society's viewpoint, this is desirable because the schools then integrate a "foreign" culture into the mainstream of American life. From the point of view of the ethnic child and his or her community, however, such a school becomes *destructive*.*

Catholic schools have one other great advantage that may explain their differential effect on the poor. By definition, the poor are powerless. Though they can sometimes obtain political power as organized groups, as *individuals* they remain powerless. To the poor who support them, these schools are examples of a way

---

* All private schools do not necessarily support the minority culture of their students nor do all public schools inevitably destroy it. The public school-Catholic school dichotomy is not precise enough for this question. Many Irish-Catholic schools, for example, did not support Italian and other Latin ethnic cultures in any full sense (although they did offer more support than the public schools would normally offer); many public schools in neighborhoods with high concentrations of Catholics are, for all practical purposes, Catholic schools. The same holds true for public schools in neighborhoods with high concentrations of other religious groups, such as Anglo-Saxon Protestants or European Jews. For these groups the experience of the public school was frequently the experience of a religious and cultural haven indistinguishable from an ethnic private school.

in which they are not powerless. The schools depend on their supporters for survival; they are the projects of the poor who pay for them. Each "project" has the effect of reordering family priorities because the project is difficult and demands sacrifice. It forces the family to put education first. The school as a project becomes the example of the power of the group, the cause of its developing power. This sense of "powerfulness" is conveyed to the children who attend the school and may be the reason for their academic achievement.

Most analysts agree that parental involvement in these schools is significantly greater, and that the commitment of the teachers and morale of the school is higher than in most inner-city public schools. But such observations, while supplying important clues, do not identify the operating reasons. The best hypothesis is that the schools are better because:

1. They are more effective community organizations than public schools. They tend to operate on community problems that are causing the children educational difficulties. They operate for much longer days than public schools, typically extending some teacher supervision of the schools until the early evening hours, and hosting meetings of community organizations through the evening.

2. They need parents' help. Without parents' contributed labor, the schools fail. Unless the parents are convinced and reinforced in their conviction that the schools are worth the tuition cost, the schools fail. Parents report they feel they are more needed and more respected by the school's professional staff. They feel their help is critical and report more satisfaction and sense of efficacy in working with the private schools. This observation by the parents is predicted by the management theory of "undermanning": understaffed organizations are more efficient because workers find satisfaction in the fact that they are critically needed and that their work makes a clear and measurable contribution to the success of the organization's enterprise. When the organization is fully staffed, the importance of an individual declines, and job satisfaction decreases. For schools, this implies that the closer they come to financial solvency, the more difficult it will be to obtain the contributed efforts needed to sustain the school's academic accomplishments.

3. They reinforce the family's view of the importance of education. Because inner-city private schools mobilize the parents so effectively, and in turn give parents evidence of the effectiveness of their efforts, these schools raise the importance of education in the hierarchy of activities to which the family heads give

70

their energies. Families tend to regard as more important activities which consume more of their time.

4. Because private schools are products of parents' and teachers' efforts—not the result of some undeserved beneficence from outside the community—they create a sense of pride in the students and parents. In sum, private schools succeed because they are close to their parents/clients and to their community. They are close to them because they need them.

Contributions to neighborhoods: Catholic inner-city schools' role in stabilizing inner-city neighborhoods has not been properly studied, but the schools are most likely an important factor. They attract and retain the most successful, and therefore the most mobile, members of the community. Indirectly they help sustain property values and encourage reinvestment, identify people who are willing to work in the community, pinpoint problems driving people from the area, and provide an arena where groups can meet to confront the problems. They offer the community a professional staff which has a stake in the survival of a particular school in a particular neighborhood (in contrast to public school staffs, which are tenured to the system, and whose schools cannot fail for lack of community support). Repeatedly, researchers have found private schools spawning extensive community activities, becoming the center of many efforts to aid the aged, the jobless, those with inadequate housing, young people, and the community as a whole.

Difference from Inner-City Public Schools

Granted that parochial schools can work closely to reinforce the family, why should this make them superior to public schools? Have they always been superior in adapting themselves, or have public schools changed? Education historians have argued that the public schools are the traditional vehicle of assimilation and upward mobility for America's immigrant population, and that the public schools have been successful in educating immigrants despite the schools' hostility to immigrant culture. Some revisionist historians argue the contrary.

In Michael Katz's view, public schools have by design been hostile to the desire of immigrant groups to assert themselves. He believes the public schools were designed to *contain* the immigrants within an industrial model of society, and that the industrial model formed the very structure of the public system. The schools impressed upon their students the distinction between workers and managers, and taught them the limits of workers. Colin Greer, in a two-pronged attack, argues: (1) that the primary purpose of the public school was to restrict the immigrants' influence—to protect American society from the "moral cesspool" created in the cities by these un-American newcomers; (2) that the schools militantly "Americanized" and put that goal before the encouragement of social mobility in the immigrant groups they served. Greer further argues that the public schools' primary goal was "Americanization," the softening of the new immigrants' impact to prevent any real changes in "native" American society. He believes the schools were interested in encouraging the new Americans to achieve only within the framework defined by the older Americans. The public schools' prime purpose, was to reduce the "threat" of the immigrants.

Diane Ravitch argues that public schools greatly benefited the immigrants, but her arguments do not actually confront Greer's. She is drawing her conclusions from a set of schools that includes "ethnic public schools," which took on the character of their ethnic groups. Greer assumes that no public schools acted in this way.

Ravitch's discussion is particularly interesting because she points out the confusion on the part of those who speak of the success of the public schools. She describes a number of schools during the period of "Americanization" and notes that some were successful; others were not. In unsuccessful schools, the immigrants' children remained "clannish" and resistant to Americanization. For Ravitch, many of the factors that we now believe contribute to the academic effectiveness of inner-city schools—particularly their adaptation and reinforcement of the ethnic family—are signs of failure. She cites an instance in which leaders of a rapidly overconcentrated Jewish section of Lower Manhattan so strongly opposed the transfer of their children to under-utilized schools in the neighboring Irish-Catholic community that the school board cancelled its transfer plans and continued to send Jewish children to overcrowded classrooms on half-day sessions.

Another observer of the New York public schools, Charles Harrington of Teachers College, recalls that as a child he believed the Jewish holidays were national holidays until he entered high school, because he had attended public elementary and junior high schools that were 98% Jewish. His schools had adapted themselves to the customs and religious practices of their neighborhood.

Both descriptions are indications that public schools once adapted themselves quite closely to their ethnic communities. This was perhaps particularly so in New York during the period of the heaviest Jewish immigrations. Generally, public schools in the past *could* mold themselves to the neighborhood they served (and let us emphasize that we are speaking of *individual* schools and the *individual* neighborhood). Whether they did mold themselves depended on the political power of the neighborhood residents. It was not until the early 1960s that the Supreme Court handed down a series of decisions prohibiting or curtailing religious practices in public schools. The Court began limiting state aid to religious schools only in the late 1940s. Up to that time— and, some have shown, even after that time—many urban public schools were able to mold themselves to their communities, even in religious practice.

Once again, the research record is not conclusive. It appears, however, that in the recent past—and certainly in the period of the great European immigrations—public schools were more able than they are today to adapt themselves to the religious and cultural practices of the people they served. At the same time, public schools more overtly pursued a mission of eradicating traces of European origin in their students, especially Latin or Slavic. Today the schools have lost much of their ethnic hostility, but they are even less able to adapt themselves to the immigrant communities. They are prohibited both by the Supreme Court's interpretation of the First Amendment and by a centralization of control over school policy in the hands of boards of education and teacher unions.

It is more difficult to differentiate neighborhood schools today than in the recent past. Private schools appear to have continued their history of serving the needs of immigrant groups, but the tradition is carried on principally in the inner-city parochial schools, which enroll disproportionate numbers of children to immigrant parents.

Are private schools divisive? The greatest fear of private schools is that they will create a society split into factions. The charge is "private schools are divisive." What is the evidence for this charge? Certainly, the emergence of armed bands from the private schools would be good evidence, but that has not happened. The critics of private schools appear most concerned that private school students will get the idea they are a priviliged group apart, better than others and with no responsibility to others. The question was most directly researched by Greeley and Rossi, who queried a sample of Catholics who had attended Catholic schools, and compared the answers to another sample of Catholics who had attended public schools. The evaluated the two populations by standard indices of racism, anti-semitism,

73

and civil-libertarianism, which are reasonably good measures of a group's attitude toward other groups, the principle which underlies the fear of "divisiveness." They found the Catholic-school-educated students less racist, less anti-semitic, and more supportive of the fundamental principle of civil liberty than their public school counterparts. (See Table 2.)

Table 2

PERCENT OF RESPONDENTS SCORING HIGH ON SOCIAL BEHAVIOR INDICES

Index	Catholics in Catholic Schools	Catholics in Public Schools
Racism	21%	25%
Anti-Semitism	30%	40%
Anti-Civil Liberties	26%	37%
N =	247	558

Note: A low score indicates a less divisive position.
Source: Table adapted from Greeley and Rossi's Table 7.1, p. 162.

Conclusion

In this chapter, we have discussed a number of purposes served by inner-city parochial schools. The schools provide improved educational opportunities for minorities; strengthen families; stabilize and organize neighborhoods; foster urban integration; force the improvement of inner-city public schools; provide religious and moral education for Catholics and non-Catholics alike; and help build parishes and extend a bridge between the church and non-Catholic minorities. Some of these purposes are traditionally Catholic, others require the church to take as its own responsibility tasks generally regarded as the province of the government. Before the church can act to preserve its inner-city schools, it must decide that these purposes are worth the cost.

Questions for Research

1. Most research on parochial schools is concerned with the degree these schools reach their own, or church objectives. Little attention has been paid to the importance of these schools in relation to public goals. It is important for researchers to begin to describe the public effects of parochial schools. It is particularly important for these descriptions to be developed at the

micro-level—specific schools in specific communities.

2. The choice presented by parochial schools over public schools is specific to each neighborhood and to each set of paroachial and public schools. The most useful studies of parochial and public schooling, from the viewpoint of policymakers, will concern how the two types of schools differ in the same neighborhoods, and with what effect for public policy goals. Studies of private schools should be matched by studies of public schools in the same neighborhoods. Research attention should be given to interaction, cooperation, and competition that may exist between the two types of schools. Which is better for a community: public and Catholic schools which are hotly competitive; those which ignore each other's presence, serving distinct subgroups within the community; or those which consciously and extensively cooperate, and help solve each other's problems? Which kind of relationship is more commonplace? These answers are likely to differ among dioceses, and even among neighborhoods within dioceses.

Notes on Sources for Chapter 3

Henry M. Brickell, *Non-Public Education in Rhode Island: Alternative for the Future*, A Study for the Special Commission to Study the Entire Field of Education, July, 1969.

John E. Coons and Stephen B. Sugarman, *Education by Choice* (Berkeley: University of California Press, 1978)

Curriculum Research and Development Center, *Public/Parochial School Project*, A Report to the Rhode Island State Department of Education, 9 vols., (Kingston, R.I.: University of Rhode Island, 1976)

John D. Donovan and George F. Madaus, *Catholic Education in the Archdiocese of Boston: The Voices of the People* (Chestnut Hill, Mass.: New England Catholic Education Center, Boston College, 1969)

Donald Erickson and George Madaus, *Issues of Aid to Non-Public Schools*, (Chestnut Hill: Boston College Center for Field Research and School Services, September, 1971)

Andrew Greeley and Peter Rossi, *The Education of Catholic Americans* (Chicago, Aldine Publishing Company, 1966)

Greg Hancock, "Public School, Parochial School: A Comparative Analysis of Governmental and Catholic Elementary Schooling in a Large City" (Unpublished Dissertation, Department of Education, University of Chicago, 1971)

Christopher Jencks, "Private Schools for Black Children," *New York Times Magazine*, November 3, 1968, pp. 30, 132-64.

Otto F. Kraushaar, *American Non-Public Schools: Patterns of Diversity* (Baltimore and London: The Johns Hopkins University Press, 1972)

Daniel U. Levine; Holly Lachowicz; Karen Oxman; Tangeman Ahden, "The Home Environment of Students in a High-Achieving Inner-city Parochial School and a Nearby Public School," *Sociology of Education,* 1972, Vol. 45, Fall, pp. 435-44.

Richard Nault, "School Affiliation and Student Commitments" *Administrators Notebook,* The University of Chicago, Midwest Administration Center, Vol. XXIV (1975-76), No. 2.

Reginal Neuwein, editor, *Catholic Schools in Action: A Study of Catholic Elementary and Secondary Schools in the U.S.* (Notre Dame and London: University of Notre Dame Press, 1966)

CHAPTER 4

REFLECTIONS ON WHAT CAN BE DONE

We will now begin this chapter with a review of the situation, and conclude with a discussion of possible solutions. Inner-city and minority Catholic schools are declining, and the decline will accelerate. If the Church follows its current approaches to aiding them, it will witness the gradual elimination of most inner-city and minority schools.

Some analysts have counseled the church to close its inner-city schools. They argue that inner-city schools enrolling high percentages of non-Catholic minorities are not parish schools in the traditional sense, do not serve the Church's needs, and are not cost-effective. They suggest that money and energy spent on them could be better spent on other inner-city activities.

Any effective attempt to aid these schools will bring changes in the church, which some will resist. As decisions about what to do are postponed, the sentiment to abandon the schools is likely to increase. The idea of closing inner-city Catholic schools is initially repugnant to most Catholics, because it goes against their habits. Catholics have long supported their schools through weekly contributions to the parish, contributions which reinforce and reaffirm their connection to the schools. But the habit of weekly giving to the schools has been broken by the separation of parish and school budgets that took place in most dioceses in the mid-1960s. The trend toward reducing parish contribution is increasing. As parishes have less stake in the day-to-day activities of the schools, parishioners' ingrained reluctance to see Catholic schools close will diminish. If the decision to aid the schools is postponed for too long, church leaders may find that Catholics believe the schools should not remain open.

The critics are correct in observing that quite often the inner-city schools are *not* supporting Catholic parishes, the traditional purpose of Catholic schools. The schools are increasingly non-Catholic; they do not attempt to convert non-Catholics to Catholicism; and they have frequently separated themselves, or been separated from, the parish. Officials have even begun to speak of two parishes—one comprising church members and the other school children and their parents—so little do the two membership groups overlap.

The critics are correct in noticing the change of purpose, but perhaps the purpose should change. Fundamentally, the question is whether the church's conception of its place in American society has changed. Does it continue to be an organization serving Catholic needs, defending its members against secular pressures to the extent of its ability? Or does it now adopt more of a public-service position?

Assuming church leaders decide it is important to preserve inner-city schools, the church can adopt one of several approaches. One means of distinguishing among the approaches is by the amount of change in the church each approach would involve. Some changes may be too severe or costly. Other changes may be extremely valuable in themselves, and may help the Church with many problems aside from those presented by the inner-city schools.

Parish Support for the School

The first option is to continue to rely on the parishes to support the schools. Catholic schools have traditionally been supported by the parish at the elementary school level, and by a combination of parish support and tuition at the high school level. In the past, this system worked very well, even for parishes of poor immigrants, because the parish population was generally large enough to support large classes, which helped keep per pupil costs down; because the ethnic immigrants frequently were able to import teaching sisters who helped reduce school costs; and because the large parish was able to spread the cost of educating the children across many families without children, or families whose children were no longer in school. Thus, the parish school was financed more like public schools, where an individual pays for the school throughout his or her taxpaying life, instead of paying a much higher bill for those few years in which he or she uses the schools.

In the inner-city this system has broken down. The population is now less concentrated. Central city Catholic schools serving three or four square block areas might have been built for a capacity of 300 students. Today the parish must serve several times that number to keep the school filled.

There are very few teaching sisters available to subsidize the costs of the inner-city schools, and the level of subsidy offered by these sisters is lower, as the expenses of the convents increase and the income-producing members decline.

In former times, Catholic schools, like public schools, could have very high pupil-teacher ratios, and still retain their reputation for quality. In recent years, however, the idea has gained currency in the education profession that schools are improved when pupil-teacher ratios are lowered. (The position is not supported by research.) Few inner-city schools can now sell the idea to parents or to their teachers that the school's quality will not suffer because of high ratios. Costs have risen proportionately.

In the inner-city in particular, parish populations declined even when school populations remained constant or increased, because many non-Catholics began residing in formerly Catholic neighborhoods and enrolling in Catholic schools. Schools with high non-Catholic enrollments normally have disproportionately low parish membership and are unable to offer substantial subsidies to the school. Average parishes provide significant subsidies to their schools: about $150 per pupil in direct cash subsidy and an additional $250 per pupil in services and supplies provided by the parish and not charged to the school's budget. Typically these latter items include fuel, maintenance, debt service, insurance, grounds landscaping, and the like. The indirect subsidy can be especially important to a school: for example, when one New York parish recently closed its school, its books showed it had been giving the school a subsidy of $20,000, approximately $120 per pupil. When the community decided to operate the school itself, the parish calculated that its real contribution to the school, including rental value of the building, had been $80,000, or about $475 per pupil.

Tuition as a Means of Supporting Inner-city Schools

When the inner-city parish is forced to reduce or end its subsidy, many parish schools have attempted to support themselves solely by tuition. Often this attempt is made without direction from the diocese and without planning. Tuition at elementary schools was introduced into most diocese in the mid-1960s. According to some reports, Catholic Church leaders made the switch in the hope of establishing (as a fact) that the schools belonged to and were operated by parents, not the Church, so that the Supreme Court could approve federal aid for the schools. Ideally, tuitions were to cover 60% of school costs, parish subsidy the remaining 40%. In the inner-city schools, the parishes did not have the income to cover even 40% of the costs. As the parish's ability to support the schools fell, the inner-city schools raised tuition.

Today, tuitions in inner-city Catholic schools are the highest in the Catholic system. As a general rule, (and some Spanish schools are notable exceptions), the lower the family income of the students, the higher the tuition the school must charge. Inner-city Catholic school tuitions normally range from $300 to $750 and fall within the top 10% of all Catholic school tuitions. We have found tuitions as high as $1,700 in schools serving predominantly lower-income populations. In the inner-city, tuitions quite frequently equal 5% to 10% of average family income.

Tuition produced both advantages and disadvantages for inner-city schools. As an advantage, it encouraged parents to take a greater role in operating the schools and solving their financial and other problems, following the principle that people take a greater interest in what they pay for directly. Tuition also lowered pastors' resistance to support the school. In the past anyone who was not a member of the parish supported the school or else non-parishioners would have a free ride at the expense of the parishioners. Pastors either refused to admit non-parishioners, or charged tuitions. Some pastors were reluctant to single out non-Catholics for tuition payments; others set the tuition prohibitively high for non-Catholics. As the principal support for the school shifted to tuition, Catholics and non-Catholics could enter on a more equal footing, each supporting the school to the same degree. Under the heading "disadvantages of tuition," we could list many of the effects already listed as "benefits." Almost immediately after its introduction, pastors realized that tuition relieved them of a great financial burden, since the school had consumed over 80% of the typical parish's income. The pastor was also relieved of demanding funds and engaging in unpleasant fund-raising activities necessary to support the school, activities which many pastors felt conflicted with their pastoral work. As the parents and the school staff became more responsible for fund-raising and paying the school's debts, they took over more of the responsibilities for managing the school. In relieving the pastor of fund-raising and administrative obligations, the change deprived the school of valuable services. Because the pastor had given the services without charge to the school budget in the past, in effect the school budget was cut when he no longer provided the services.

In opening the school to non-Catholics—and especially in relaxing the requirement that all students receive basic religious instruction and practice the Catholic religion—tuition encouraged a rift between many traditional pastors and their own school administrators. Quite a few pastors withdrew their support of inner-city schools when they decided that the purpose of the parish school was to educate Catholics, and that their school—with its high non-Catholic enrollments and relaxed Catholic curricular requirements—no longer served this need.

Tuition created financial hardships for some parents in a number of ways. Traditionally, the entire parish made contributions to the school and saw the school as a parish obligation. Those with higher incomes contributed more. Parents could pay according to their means. But because general family expenses rise as children reach school age, lower-income parents face greater financial strain when their children enter school. Frequently, these parents would actually lower their parish contributions during this period even though their children were in school. They could send their children to the school "tuition free" without calling special attention to themselves by seeking aid from the parish school board, principal or pastor. The imposition of tuition made this impossible, and many lower-income parents refused to send their children to the school because they would not accept charity. In other cases, parishes refused to enroll parents who could not pay the tuition.

One example of this problem is quite striking. In 1967, Catholic schools in one Louisiana diocese were ordered integrated by the bishop. In one small town, two schools—one white and one black—were joined, and the parents elected a school board to operate the combined schools. The white parish school had traditionally charged tuition, $150 per student. The black school had been a free "mission" school. The board instituted the tuition for the combined school, which prevented almost all the black students from enrolling.

Finally, the imposition of tuition directly raised educational costs for parents. Parishioners can deduct money given to the church from gross income in figuring their taxable income for federal, state and local taxes. But they cannot now deduct tuition payments from gross income, and all governments now charge taxes on income spent for tuition to elementary and secondary schools. The imposition of tuition raised the costs of Catholic education substantially. The increase ranged from 15% to over 100% of the parish's school costs, depending on state taxes and the individual taxpayer's tax bracket. The impact was particularly great on inner-city parents because their tuitions were higher and their incomes lower.

Inner-city schools quickly reach a point where tuition increases force some parents to withdraw students from the school, and deter others from enrolling. Then the schools reach their limits; increases in tuition actually produce less revenue because enrollments drop. Tuitions are important to inner-city schools, but the schools also require subsidy.

School Co-ops to Reduce Expenses: Inner-city parishes have overcome some financial problems by requiring parents to make in-kind payments to the school, which relieve the school of direct expenses. It is common for parents and other parishioners to paint or repair the school building. In several Southern California Mexican-American parishes, the parents actually constructed the school buildings. In addition to these extraordinary efforts, schools may regularly require parents to work in the lunch room, playground or library, serve as teacher aids or helpers in the secretary's office, drive the school bus or clean the halls. In most inner-city schools, parents actually teach classes, frequently for little or no pay. Many inner-city schools require parents to raise funds through school raffles and festivals, or to pay higher tuitions.

Inner-city schools must develop close connections with parents to obtain needed services. Parents who work with the teachers are more knowledgeable about the school's problems than parents in the more traditional Catholic school, where the operation of the school is left entirely to the teaching sisters. A cooperative school normally requires a much more consultive and participatory relationship with the parents, and consequently modifies its governing structure, thus encouraging parents to assume responsibility for the school.

General consideration: Inner-city Catholic schools are either self-supporting, or must be subsidized by outsiders. If supported by Catholic church groups, they would be financed by the bishop's central treasury or by other parishes. In the latter case there is really no choice, since churches run very few profit-making enterprises. The funds the bishop can redistribute to inner-city schools must be contributed by wealthier Catholics. Other outsiders—the people in the community in which the school operates, foundations or the government—might also help support the school.

Before considering more carefully the various alternatives, we should notice some characteristics of school subsidies, especially those from outside the parish, that will affect the success of any inner-city aid plan. Subsidies are grants to schools or parishes which pay some portion of the school expenses, so that the amount which must be raised by tuition can be reduced. Subsidies are necessary when tuitions rise beyond the reach of a significant number of those who would like to attend the school. When there are no subsidies, and tuitions rise, the schools reach a point where their tuitions deter parents from enrolling their children. The higher the tuition, the fewer parents who can afford the school. Eventually tuition increases are counterproductive because the increased revenue from the higher tuitions is offset by a decline in the number of enrolled students. For example, one South Bronx Catholic school with 300 students enrolled found that it would have a deficit in the second half of its school year unless it raised tuitions by $50 per pupil—tuition rose from $100 to $150 for the half year. The school lost 80 students in the second semester, and the resulting loss of tuition left the school with a greater deficit than it had before it increased tuition. A school subsidy, which in the end was required to pay school bills, would have left the school in substantially better financial condition.

This example teaches us another lesson about subsidies. Although the specific school would have benefited from a more timely subsidy, the Catholic inner-city schools in its neighborhood would have been adversely affected. Most of the students who left the school switched to other nearby Catholic schools with lower tuitions and more stable futures. Most of the switching was by non-Catholic students, who were not members of the parish (generally commuting to the school from nearby parishes, attracted by the good education at a low tuition), and so not tied to the parish school. As inner-city populations have declined and Catholic schools have found themselves with vacant seats, and as more non-Catholics have enrolled to fill the empty places, the Catholic inner-city schools have practically abandoned the practice of assigning children to Catholic schools according to the location of their residence. This practice has lead to a new competition for students among some Catholic inner-city schools. Subsidies may upset the terms of this competition, keeping tuitions unnecessarily low even in nearby schools with no gain to the Catholic schools. On the other hand, Catholic schools would gain from subsidies if lower tuition enabled parents to transfer their children to Catholic schools.

Subsidy by a Wealthy Parish, or by the Diocese: Dioceses have attempted to help subsidize inner-city parishes by linking wealthier parishes to the inner-city ones in need of financial help, or by taxing the wealthier parishes to provide funds for distribution to the inner-city parishes. With either type of approach, dioceses have sought voluntary participation, or have attempted to order the participation of the parishes and their members. Voluntary approaches appear to have been more successful than more authoritative attempts, but is difficult to gauge their success clearly since many voluntary approaches are unmonitored by central authorities. Chicago asked its wealthier parishes to adopt inner-city parishes in need of help. The diocese attempted to link the parishes closely by encouraging exchange of priests, cooperation between the parish organizations, and joint activities. The diocese has not monitored the degree of exchange between the parishes involved, but there are some indications of success. The project has created some enthusiasm among parishioners.

The Brooklyn diocese ordered a more drastic conjoining of parishes, in which it assigned parishes into membership in a "parish cluster" and created a governing structure for the cluster. Wealthier parishes were expected to help cover the deficits of the parishes in the cluster to which they were assigned. The cluster concept worked well to encourage inner-city parishes to pool their assets, combine schools, and in other ways cooperate with each other to reduce costs. In practice, wealthier parishes failed to participate. Their participation was particularly difficult to order since it required the voluntary attendance of lay members at cluster meetings. The clusters did not increase revenues for the inner-city.

The New York and St. Louis dioceses levied a small tax on their wealthier parishes, and requested voluntary contributions for the purpose of aiding inner-city schools. The programs are modest in size, (New York has insufficient funds to cover the school needs) but must be regarded at least as moderate successes, especially when compared to the experience of Detroit, where the archbishop attempted to order suburban parishes to help support the inner-city schools. Church contributions dropped dramatically, and the effort failed.

Overall, the record is poor. Most dioceses have been unable to raise sufficient revenue to prevent inner-city school closings. As the burden of these schools increases, the situation grows worse. Catholics are contributing smaller portions of their personal wealth to church purposes, and church revenues, after considering the effects of inflation, are declining.

In commenting on the church's financial plight, some argue that the level of Catholic giving has increased but has been outstripped by increasing parish costs, leaving a diminishing proportion of funds for redistribution to inner-city schools. Parish expenses *have* risen with inflation and with the decline in teaching orders whose labor has subsidized the schools. In constant dollars, contributions have declined. The decline is particularly important, because in the last two decades the rise in Catholic church members' private incomes has superseded inflation. As individuals, Catholics have substantially increased their economic and political power.

Today's Catholics are no longer primarily immigrants. Catholics form 25% of the U.S. population. After Jews, Irish and

Italian Catholics have the highest incomes of all ethnic groups, are rapidly taking their places in the professions, and hold many of the positions of power in our society. Catholics have held the highest public and private offices. Their election to governorships and Senate seats has become commonplace. Within a decade, Catholics have become presidents of the United States, General Motors, ITT, and one of the oldest Protestant private colleges, Columbia University. All of these factors are effects of a decline in anti-Catholicism. In turn, Catholics as a group have lost their siege mentality. The church has been unable, however, to tap the rising income of its members to support inner-city schools adequately. Its failure reflects not bad intentions of wealthier Catholics, but the inadequacy of diocesan political and financial organizations to meet the conditions that have evolved in the cities.

The Problems of Parish Organization: The most serious organizational problems are presented by the parishes. The parish structure focuses the attention of wealthier parishioners on their own parish's immediate problems. If parishes could be reorganized so that the parishioners felt the same responsibility toward the members of the lowest-income parishes (in other words, if distinctions among parishes could be obliterated) the church would obtain the revenues necessary to support inner-city schools.

Let us examine the problem a little more closely. Parishes are parochial, a word which means "in the vicinity of the home." The closest American equivalent is neighborhood. The church has organized itself on a neighborhood basis, and each neighborhood is responsible for its own affairs. Each neighborhood stands on its own. The corollary is that parishes do not frequently take on their neighbors' problems and responsibilities.

The approach has been effective in ethnic American communities, for it reinforces self-sufficiency. It was a valuable attribute at a time when American Nativists were fearful that the lower-class culture of the Irish, Latins, and Slavs, and the politics of the Italians, Poles, and other immigrants would contaminate the American culture. Outside help would not come to these neighborhoods. The success of the parishes increased the political power of Catholics. The parish was integral to the rise of Catholic groups.

The parish structure is strongly supported. Parishioners feel responsible for their own problems, not for the problems of other parishes. It is not that a sense of charity does not exist; some parishes are indeed quite generous to others, but there is no sense of obligation comparable to the obligation parishioners feel toward their own parish.

The parish structure divorces the wealthy from the poor

To compound the problem, now that they have gained social status and have the income to support their schools without great efforts, the wealthier Catholics have lost most of their reasons for supporting Catholic schools.

• As Catholics' social status has risen, they have become more politically powerful and have gained control of public systems. Consequently, they have lost the sense that these institutions are being imposed on them by outsiders—a sense that was among the driving impulses generating the Catholic system.

• As Catholics concentrate in greater proportions in the suburbs surrounding major cities, they will come into control of more public systems. When a high percentage of a public school system's board, staff and students are Catholic, the factors distinguishing the system from the Catholic schools disappear. The reasons for supporting separate Catholic schools are not obvious. If Catholic schools are not necessary to defend the faith, why have them?

• From their own experiences, wealthy parishes will find less reason to support Catholic schools in general. They will increasingly feel that the Church's commitment to their own schools is lessening. Many wealthier parishes in new, suburban communities have not been permitted to build or expand their schools. Many others have suffered a loss of some religious instructors and maybe even a pull-out of the teaching order, because they were regarded as too wealthy to need the teaching subsidy.*

---

* The church itself has seemed to tell upper-income Catholics that Catholic schools are less important. Virtually no new Catholic schools have been built since the mid-1960s. In only seven years—from 1967 to 1973—the number of suburban Catholic schools declined by 17%, and suburban and small town Catholic schools by 22%. In this same period, Catholic populations of suburbs and small towns increased dramatically. A good conservative guess would be that Catholic suburban population increased at least 50% in that period, an increase subject to obvious regional variations.

Perhaps as serious as the movement to the suburbs has been the inter-regional population movement from the Northeast and Midwest to the Southwest and West, from areas with 74% of all Catholic schools to areas with only 15% of the Catholic schools. Because the migration has taken place during the period when Catholic ethnic groups were rising to high positions on the socioeconomic ladder, it is likely that Catholics were a substantial component of this migration. Once again, Catholics were moving to areas where there are too few Catholic schools to serve them. To add to the irony, it is the very parishes these migrants have left behind that are now inner-city parishes in need of help. The poverty of these urban and inner-city parishes has helped frustrate the diocesan building program.

• Educated Catholics have witnessed theologians arguing that Catholic schools are unnecessary and are not the primary work of the parish.

• Wealthy Catholics' reasons for supporting inner-city schools would also be frustrated: inner-city schools themselves are *not* pursuing conversions. One attractive reason to support inner-city schools would have been to further the growth of the church among black and Spanish minorities who are inactive Catholics. But the Church has practically abandoned efforts at conversion, and is particularly embarrassed by its former attempts to convert children.

Democratization of Authority: The problem is even more difficult than we have previously explained. Once the church could overcome these problems simply by ordering wealthy parishes to support inner-city schools. Today, the church is far less able simply to order compliance. The rise in social status of leading Catholic groups has weakened the traditional hierarchical structure of the church. Today, parishioners must be given greater independence in deciding whether or not to aid inner-city schools. The new higher-status Catholics will not accept directives of the church hierarchy on the question, which would have been accepted by their grandparents, just as they no longer follow, as bloc voters, the political leadership of the tightly disciplined urban political parties. The laity and the religious will have to be consulted on any new policy directives for the church. The church leadership can no longer win obedience from higher-status Catholics merely on the basis of tradition and their position within the church.

Furthermore, it will be more difficult for the church leadership to win agreement because higher-status Catholics have much more education than their parents. To some extent the authority of the pastor as the moral leader of his parish has rested on his expertise, but the higher-status Catholic's professional training or advanced education tends to undermine the parish priest's traditional authority. It is not that a parish of higher-status Catholics cannot be powerful and accomplish many things, but that what these parishioners do cannot be decided unilaterally by the bishop or the pastor. Inevitably, the parishes will become more democratic in their operation, in much the same way that political parties have become more democratic in policy setting and candidate selection.

Not only have Catholics gained status, but the laity and religious have gained more authority within the policy-setting arenas of the church. Even if their greater authority has not been granted formally, it exists as a practical matter. Without the agreement of the laity, the church is powerless.

The Problem of Protecting the Independence and Self-Reliance of the Inner-City Parish School: If the church succeeds in restructuring its parishes so that the wealthier parishes have the same sense of obligation toward the inner-city parishes that they have toward their own schools, it still faces serious problems because of the parish structure. Adequate revenues *will be* forthcoming. But the church cannot change the wealthier parishes' sense of financial responsibility without also changing their sense of political responsibility: parishes are used to having a voice in how their contributions are spent, and the contributors will expect a similar voice once their sense of "parish" has been properly expanded. At the most elemental level, if their funds are absolutely necessary to the operation of the inner-city schools, they will have to participate in deciding what those schools will be like and how they will operate. The wealthy will have to become interested in those schools, and will have to agree in general with what the schools are doing, or they will not give their support.

If the funds are collected by the diocese, and distributed by central authorities to the inner-city schools, the parishioners contributing the funds will gain a role in the deliberations at that level. If the funds go directly from a wealthier to a poorer parish, the contributors will become influential at the parish level.

If the church relies on direct parish-to-parish aid, or on aid which flows from wealthier parishes through the church's central diocesan offices to the poorer parishes, we should expect several changes in the way the church forms its policies—political changes affecting the central diocesan offices. In essence, the attempt to finance inner-city schools will force the church to abandon parochialism, a principle that has served the church well by allowing it to encompass and satisfy disparate groups because it has imposed relatively few diocesan rules on its parishes. However, it is likely that this principle will be abandoned in any event, for a number of reasons having little to do with attempts to aid inner-city schools. The inner-city school aid question will only speed up an already occurring process. Let us review the changes in the church's policy-making structures most concerned with education.

Bishops commonly have treated parishes on a case-by-case basis, permitting some to do what is not done elsewhere, keeping in close contact with some and permitting others to proceed substantially on their own. For some purposes, the resulting lack of uniformity is a disadvantage—it does make it harder to guarantee equitability in the opportunity given Catholics to enroll their children in Catholic schools, but it also permits a system highly adaptive to local idiosyncrasies, and capable of supporting a diversity of cultural heritages. This characteristic of Catholic dioceses virtually requires the chanceries to be secretive about their activities with parishes, to prevent the administrators and laity of one parish from comparing their treatment to what is given others.

Bishops once directed Catholic education through parish pastors when the pastors were the principal organizers and managers of the schools. However, a number of factors have reduced the pastor's pre-eminence in favor of the teaching orders and the laity, and the line of authority connecting the bishops to their schools necessarily has changed. The first challenge to the pastor's role came as a result of the rise of educational expertise in the teaching orders, and the consequent increase in their scarcity value. When teaching sisters were plentiful and relatively untrained, the pastor would discount the value of their contributed services. As they became more highly trained professionally, and their numbers fell, the real value of the subsidy they gave the schools increased. The orders required a kind of payment for their increased professionalism in increased authority over the schools rather than in increased salary. Pastors began to defer to religious orders on matters of school policy. This transfer of responsibility gained momentum. Pastors learned that the religious could relieve them of substantial burdens, and increasingly desired to give the religious full responsibility for the schools.

Bishops, simply to retain their traditional influence over the operation of the schools, began to establish diocesan offices and boards of education. Most typically, the first boards were composed of representatives of the teaching orders from the elementary and high school levels, and representatives of the parishes and the chancery. The superintendents of education were established to be *professional* rather than hierarchical leaders of the system. Often the superintendents were selected from one of the diocesan teaching orders, but almost always the superintendent was chosen for his or her recognized educational leadership. These two relatively recent innovations, diocesan boards and superintendents, permitted the bishops to reestablish—although in altered form—their organizational connection to those operating the schools.

As lay teachers became a more important component of the system, and parish school boards or councils became their formal employers, the diocesan boards expanded again to include greater proportions of these new groups in their members, and dioceses began to appoint laity as superintendents of their systems. The increase in lay staffing is perhaps the most portentous shift in the organizational structure of the church in recent times: two-thirds of all Catholic school teachers are lay, and perhaps as many as 25% of these, including the principals of some schools, are non-Catholics. In many schools, no religious teachers are on the staff. As the religious staff of the schools declined, pastors increasingly handed responsibility for the schools to lay parish councils and school boards. Lay teachers have no traditional bonds of obedience to the bishops, and are not a regular part of the traditional bureaucratic structure of the church. The bishops have no direct correspondence with lay boards, and their position in the church's hierarchial structure is ambiguous. The new central offices of education, and the expanded diocesan boards of education, were necessary innovations to retain diocesan influence over the operation of the schools.

These changes are relatively easy to understand if they are viewed simply as diocesan attempts to establish a dialogue between the bishop, the formal governor of the diocese, and the effective administrators of the local schools. Obviously, the rise in importance of religious as parish school directors was serious. A bishop has far less communication with a teaching order serving a parish school than with a pastor who serves as school administrator. The change to a lay faculty and administration is an even more serious change, since the laity do not vow obedience to the bishop, and his authority over them is moral and principally persuasive.

If the central diocesan offices gain control of substantial amounts of funds to be used to support the elementary schools, they will begin to establish rules for those schools, and to manage them, in ways similar to their control over diocesan high schools. The diocese tends to treat all high schools relatively equally; it will be aiding and enforcing its measures only on inner-city elementary schools.

Most dioceses set rules that all schools are expected to follow, but have extremely limited ability in enforcing them. Of course, rules established by the (arch)bishop are more completely and consistently followed than those established by the school office or board, because the (arch)bishop has substantial powers for enforcing his position, and the school offices do not. The aid the diocese distributes to inner-city schools can become a means for enforcing diocesan rules. The diocese will have to discipline itself not to enforce rules on "aided" schools that it is not enforcing on others. That will be almost impossible to do since some rules will directly affect subsidies.

The diocese may create a rule-making body, such as a school board, which includes parish representatives. In this case, however, the diocese must face the question of who is the proper representative of the parish—the pastor, the principal, a member of the parish school board, etc. It is likely that the proper representative will differ from one parish to another.

Overall, sufficient aid for inner-city schools will come at the cost of weakened parish structures in the wealthier parishes because those contributing funds will become involved in responsibilities and decisions beyond the confines of their parish, and also in the inner-city parishes because the pastors and other leaders will become subject to greater outside direction. We have some experience which suggests this latter trend.

Subsidies of inner-city schools are not new. Beginning parishes were traditionally subsidized in a number of ways. One, close to the twinning approach followed in the inner-city in Chicago, had the parent parish provide an initial grant, like a dowry, to a new parish formed in a portion of its former territory. Or, in a approach actually used to aid inner-city schools as well as other parishes, bishops would consult with pastors of fledging or weak parishes to work out special arrangements permitting the parish to avoid diocesan imports. Occasionally, the bishops would contribute directly to the parish income.

When school budgets were separated from parish budgets in the early 1960s, some bishops continued to aid the school by contributing to the parish budget. This approach became more difficult for three reasons: bishops found it more difficult to make the additions in secret, since the parishes were required to make public reports of their financing; diocesan school boards began to express concern over the decisions of which schools to aid and how much aid to give them; and in the inner-city, the fortunes of the school were so separated from those of the parish, that aid to the parish did not reach the school. In many cases, the parish made no regular contribution to the school, and the parish administrators were unaware of most of the problems and needs of the schools. Bishops gradually turned to their school boards to guide them in subsidizing inner-city schools.

The rise of the school boards challenged the traditional authority of the pastor. Logically, a school board would need to see the budget of both parish and school before it could award funds either to the parish or directly to the school. The board would need assurances from the pastor that the centrally contributed schools funds would be used for the school budget and that the parish would not withdraw its own subsidies to its school. Pastors were required to report and discuss their finances with boards composed primarily of sisters and lay persons.*

We should expect the impact of increased funding of inner-city schools through diocesan efforts to increase changes in the pastor's position, and to fragment further the structure of the parish. Although aid may be needed for those schools, changes likely to accompany it may be damaging.

Importance of Local Authority and Responsibility to the Inner-City School: We should not underestimate the importance of this potential damage. Inner-city schools can succeed only if the parish can enlist parents to support the schools. The schools are most successful when the parish can enlist the aid of other neighborhood residents, not just parish members, and also improve the neighborhood. This is especially important in heavily non-Catholic inner-city neighborhoods. Parishes with substantial non-Catholic school enrollments have more difficulty making a connection to the community, a difficulty which increases if they are subject to significant interference from diocesan or other parish sources supplying the subsidies.

Compare inner-city schools with non-Catholic enrollments to a lower-income ethnic parish. When an ethnic parish has an all-Catholic school, the parish normally is a relatively tight-knit community. The pastor and parishioners know a great deal about one another. Catholic parishioners are regularly informed about the activities, problems and needs of the school and the church, and are enlisted in its aid, through announcements and sermons

---

* The problem of preventing a local government—in this case the parish—from reducing its previous level of support as outside funds arrive is one of the most difficult to resolve. The federal government has encountered the problem in its ESEA, Title 1, program. It found that local school districts put ESEA funds into the target inner-city schools, and then took out of those schools local tax levy money to give to schools out of the target area. The federal government evolved the principle of comparability: The local school system must show that it is expending its funds equally among all schools before the federal money is distributed within the system. Comparability has had a profound effect on public school operations. A similar principle is likely to evolve in the parishes: Pastors will have to show they are distributing parish revenues across all expense categories relatively evenly, so that the centrally distributed money to aid inner-city education does not, in the end, aid some other activity, such as a neighborhood housing council or the needed renovation of a church hall.

at weekly Mass. In essence, there exists in the parish a bond of trust between parishioner and school or parish administrator. Parishioners believe that decisions affecting the school and the parents are in the best interest of the parish. In Catholic schools, formal mechanisms for governing the schools, like school boards, serve more the purpose of increasing parental efforts on the school's behalf, than obtaining parental agreement or confidence in the school. School boards are established primarily to give parents responsibility for difficult problems the schools face, like financing, tuition collection, planning and construction, safety in the neighborhood, public improvements in the area, and the like. Even in the absence of a parish school board or council, the pastor will find it comparatively easy to mobilize parishioners to meet neighborhood or school problems.

Non-Catholic, School Board, and School Policies: When non-Catholics are involved in the school, a formal mechanism in communication must be established, because there is no regular, daily contact between the non-Catholic and the priests and teachers of the school.* Otherwise, school policy will not reflect the feelings and interests of non-Catholics, and the schools will not receive as much assistance from non-Catholic parents. In some extreme cases non-Catholics bring to the Catholic school an attitude learned from public schools: "the squeaky wheel gets the oil." This attitude is especially prevalent in inner-city areas, where parents may expect that they will have to demonstrate and protest their unhappiness in order to be heard. Some Catholic schools with substantial non-Catholic enrollments have gone so far as to appoint boards of trustees from the local business community, and others have elected school boards in public neighborhood elections.

Non-Catholics present special difficulties to a Catholic schcol's approach to religious instruction and practice. Many non-Catholics are in Catholic schools because they have no other acceptable choices for the education of their children. Consequently, we can find a wide range of religions in Catholic schools: Taoist, Buddhist, Jewish, Seventh-Day-Adventist, Mormons, and Jehovah's Witnesses. Inner-city parishes have approached the education of these children in different ways. Some have encouraged non-Catholic enrollment; others have made their attendance onerous. As a practical matter, there is no church position on the education of non-Catholic children, and no consistent diocesan policy is followed. Schools adopt the policies desired by their

---

* Unless the school adopts the position of one Chicago parish and requires non-Catholic parents to attend Catholic Mass and instruction.

leaders—priests, religious or lay. There appears to be at least three distinct approaches.

1. **The traditional Catholic parish approach:** Many parishes insist on a traditional approach. They instruct *all* children in Catholicism and require all to participate in the Mass and other Catholic celebrations. Conversions may or may not be encouraged. This approach is repellent to some fundamentalists and Jehovah's Witnesses, who do not enroll in "traditional" schools. However, it has certain advantages. It strengthens parish structure, and does not force the parish to question whether the school is sufficiently central to its purposes to warrant the extraordinary financial support so often required in inner-city areas.

2. **The mission school and witness school approach:** Some parishes have adopted the support of the school as a means of bearing Christian witness and attempt to convert non-Catholics. Often these schools are supported by societies or other sources of outside funding. Frequently they serve non-Catholics with extra ordinarily disparate backgrounds: native Hawaiian, Micronesian, and Oriental plantation workers on Molokai; Koreans in San Francisco; Chinese in Philadelphia; Zuni or Navajo Indians on their respective reservations; Aleuts in northern Alaska; and blacks in rural Louisiana. Typically, these schools adapt themselves to the religious beliefs of the people they serve, forming an amalgam of Catholic principles, beliefs, and traditions of the people.

3. **The ecumenical parish approach:** Some parishes have moderated sectarian Catholicism into a general Christian and moral concern. They accommodate many religions and often require some religious—but not necessarily Catholic—practice. They frequently do not have any formal religious instruction or daily practice in the schools.

In considering non-Catholics in Catholic schools, we must be careful not to assume that the parents have no religious objectives in choosing these schools. In a recent study of non-Catholic parents in Catholic schools, we found parents highly supportive of Catholic religious education. The moral authority offered by the church was strongly desired; it was more important to non-Catholics than to Catholics in many areas. Non-Catholic blacks, in particular, frequently made no distinctions between Christian sects, and valued the Catholic schools for their Christian training.

Many inner-city Catholic schools enrolling large numbers of non-Catholic students have substantially de-emphasized Catholic instruction, and have severed close connection with their parish. This damages the school in two important ways. First, in separating from the parish, the school relieves the pastor of the obligation of being full-time manager and fund-raiser. Even parishes with no Catholic membership, and therefore with no regular subsidy from the parish to the school, find the pastor's fund-raising efforts extremely important. Schools that no longer advance his pastoral mission must take second place in his priorities. Although there is an element of "good works" in maintaining Catholic schools that have lost their Catholic character, other pastoral priorities must often supersede these efforts.

Second, the school that is less connected to the parish is less connected to the community. Parish organizations bring the school wider support in the community, and facilitate a community-wide attack on neighborhood problems which affect the academic fortunes of parish children. Without parish support (unless the school simply duplicates parish efforts to organize the neighborhood) the school is in danger of becoming, an isolated entity operating exclusively between 8:30 and 3:30 each day, and closing its doors to community problems which affect the educational opportunities of the children.

Christian Parish Schools

Some parishes have connected themselves so closely to the community that they have left the parish structure altogether. Some have severed all formal connection with the church, such as the CORE Community School in the South Bronx (once Our Lady of Victory). Others have remained connected to the church, but seek substantial public support, such as the Milwaukee association of inner-city schools, called The Central City Grade School Program, and C/U/E/S, a consortium of community schools, formerly inner-city Catholic schools, publicly supported in Kansas City, Kansas. Some black inner-city parishes, in attempting to link themselves more closely to the community, and to obtain support from the area, have adopted a public school model. The school has established a school board elected from the neighborhood, in regular public polling places, with all neighborhood residents eligible to vote. Candidates are selected on the basis of their interest in preserving the neighborhood—such as local business persons, Protestant clergy, block organization captains and the like. However, the schools usually must levy very high tuitions, for they have not been able to get substantial numbers of non-parents (community residents who benefit from the school's presence but do not use its services) to help support the school. The schools have begun a process of divorcing themselves from parish affairs and have not been able to mobilize other parish organizations for support.

The loss of Catholic religious character may lessen the importance of Catholic schools to non-Catholics. Traditionally, the parish is a community of believers, and the school reflects and supports that belief, and also serves to make the parish members community leaders in the next generation. Concern for the future shape of the community—a concern intimately connected with morality and religious belief—provides the motivation for non-parents to support the parish schools. Two important differences set inner-city Catholic schools apart from public schools: they avowedly believe in and provide a moral order for their students, and they are community schools—extensions of the home.

Interviews with non-Catholic parents of children in inner-city Catholic schools have repeatedly found that the parents value the schools for their religious character. In my own studies, I have found non-Catholics to be more supportive of the "Catholic" character of the schools than Catholic parents. One explanation for this anomalous position is that Baptists and other Protestants sending their children to inner-city schools do not believe sectarian differences are important, and see Catholics simply as Christians.* Repeatedly I have found that parents respect these schools as Christian, and that teaching Catholicism to non-Catholic Christians is a greater problem for the Catholic teachers and administrators than for the families.

Witness on this matter, the behavior of the most successful Catholic inner-city school, Chicago's Holy Angels School. Approximately 40% of its students admit to being non-Catholic. The school has 1,300 students and a waiting list of 300, but the church has only 800 active members. The school instructs all students in Catholicism ("We are a catholic school."), requires their participation in religious services (non-Catholics may bring a letter from a Protestant minister attesting to their participation elsewhere), and requires the parents of non-Catholic children to attend instruction. "We emphasize parental responsibility. These parents must know what their children are being taught."

The parish actively converts new parishioners, averaging about 75 converts a year. It is described as "a Polish-Catholic parish," by outsiders, "except it's black." The parents do not agree with some of the religious policies of the school—especially those requiring attendance and instruction, but they have no

---

* The reason even fits Oriental parents—principally Buddhists and Taoists—sending their children to Catholic schools serving Oriental areas of mainland U.S. cities and Hawaii. In this case, the parents express respect for the schools concern with God and the moral order.

choice. The parish administrators explain that they attempted a voluntary approach, but the parish and school began to falter. "We are relatively authoritarian because that is a necessary condition of our survival."

Catholic schools which insist non-Catholic students receive religious instruction can cause some difficulties for adherents of some religions. Jehovah's Witnesses in both Chicago and New York reported that religious doctrinal conflicts—principally over the Jehovah's Witness' belief that only 144,000 elect are saved—forced them to withdraw their children from Catholic schools. In teaching a more doctrinal Catholicism, the inner-city Catholic schools will reach fewer non-Catholic students.

The inner-city schools must get greater support from their communities. One solution is to use them as instruments for increasing the size of the parishes. One obstacle to this is the legacy of sectarian differences which isolate non-Catholic Christians from Catholic parishes, even while Catholics have become embarrased over open ambitions at conversion. One potential solution would be the development of more open Christian parishes in the inner-city, perhaps involving the affiliation of some large groups of Protestant inner-city pastors. Conversion is a slow process, and the inner-city parishes need some means of permitting large numbers of Protestant and other religious inner-city families to share the responsibilities for supporting inner-city Catholic schools, just as they have already sought out the benefits of academic quality, safety and moral life which these schools offer. If this happens, the church will find that it will also have to share responsibility for governing the inner-city schools with other churches and community organizations. How can it share responsibility without relinquishing so much influence and control that it is no longer interested in supporting the schools? What arrangements can be made with other churches and how can other churches in the inner-city be encouraged to help support the inner-city Catholic schools? Cooperative church ventures may save some inner-city schools, but may also simply reduce the variety of religious schools available to inner-ciy residents. Would this latter change be in the church's interests?

We have seen that the church faces increasing difficulty in maintaining its inner-city schools, and that the schools are extremely important to future minority membership in the American Church. We have seen that the inner-city Catholic schools aid the nation in achieving a number of important public goals, including the integration of cities, the improvement of educational opportunity for minorities, the improvement of inner-city neighborhoods, and the establishment of aid to families who attempt to provide moral direction for their children.

In this chapter we have reviewed a number of approaches for assisting inner-city schools, and discussed some of the political changes each new approach fosters or requires for its success. We have not attempted to argue that any one approach is best, and should be adopted. Selecting among the approaches requires that we first determine the most important purposes that inner-city schools should serve. Will the church support schools which do not directly increase its membership? Will it support schools which primarily serve public purposes? Does it wish to change its relationship to non-Catholics, and establish ways of involving them in church organizations?

Selecting among the approaches also requires that we decide what changes within its own organizational structure the church wishes to encourage or avoid, for each approach carries with it some organizational changes.

If the church continues to proceed as it has, in effect making decisions by not making decisions, it will lose its inner-city schools, lose the important contribution it can make through these schools to ameliorate the social and economic differences developing in America, and lose its most important connection to blacks and other minorities.

Questions for Research

1. What are the various ways in which Catholic parishes have connected themselves to those living within their boundaries? Which have proven most effective when the neighborhood has a high percentage of non-Catholic residents?

2. The church must resolve its mission in the inner-city. Is there a means of accepting Baptists, Seventh Day Adventists, and members of other Protestant sects into the active life of the Catholic parish, in such a way that the parish can begin to support its own schools? Non-Catholics frequently seek out Catholic schools for their Christian, moral instruction. How important are sectarian differences to the operation of the schools? Can the church more energetically attempt the conversion of new Catholics in the inner-city? What symbols of the church's connection to minority groups must be developed?

Appendix A

EXAMINING THE DIFFERENCES BETWEEN PUBLIC AND PAROCHIAL EDUCATION: THE RHODE ISLAND EXPERIENCE

David S. Morton, Ph.D., Assistant Professor *

In the fall of 1976, the Rhode Island Board of Regents, the governing body for Education in the state, was presented once again with information from the Statewide Testing Program which indicated parochial school students outperformed public school students on the Iowa Test of Basic Skills at both the 4th and 8th grades. In a state where 65% of the population is Catholic and nearly 25% of the student population attends parochial schools, information indicating parochial schools were consistently out-scoring public schools on a standardized test had received a great deal of publicity. Each year newspapers throughout the state publicized the results. The subsequent public concern was reflected in the numerous hours the Board of Regents spent discussing the issue.

In response to public criticism, the Board of Regents directed the Rhode Island Department of Education to seek assistance with a private contractor to design and execute a research study identifying the factors accounting for the differences in the standardized achievement test scores between public and parochial school students.

The contractor was asked to submit a proposal which would address one primary question:

Why do parochial school students, especially at the eighth grade level, tend to perform better than public school students in relation to the national norms on the Iowa Test of Basic Skills?

A group of researchers associated with the University of Rhode Island's Curriculum Research and Development Center (CRDC) was contracted to undertake the study. CRDC focused the study on three areas: school setting factors, population fac-

* The following individuals contributed to this reasearch work: Barbara Brittingham, Ph.D., Patricia Ewing, M.A., Stephen Horwitz, Ph.D., William Hunter, Ph.D., John Long, Ph.D., and Thomas R. Pezzullo, Ph.D.

tors, and psychometric/test intrinsic factors. Four data sources were used:

(1) *Iowa Test of Basic Skills* (ITBS)—examination of the administration, use, and attitudes toward the standardized test;

(2) *Parent attitudes*—examination of the attitudes of parents toward educational policies of the school, and their interest in their children's education;

(3) *Organizational aspects*—exploration of the organizational environment within the school including teacher perceptions of students and teacher morale; and

(4) *Curriculum and instruction*—examination of the curricular and instructional activities undertaken in the school.

Data for examination of the school setting and population factors were collected by two means: interviews with classroom teachers and administrators at building and central administration levels, and a short questionnaire administered to classroom teachers. Schools selected for interviews included two of each of the fourth and eighth grades:

(1) high achieving public

(2) low achieving public

(3) high achieving parochial

(4) low achieving parochial

A semi-structured interview form was developed and field-tested for use in the interview process. For each school selected, at least five classroom teachers from different grade levels, the building administrator, and personnel from the central office administration were interviewed. The short form questionnaire was developed to elicit information in specified areas from the remaining teachers in each school who were not interviewed.

The examination of the impact of psychometric and test-intrinsic factors upon the analysis and interpretation of the data focused upon two areas:

(1) *General Scaling Issues*—Examination of certain inherent characteristics of the ITBS, its normative information, and various problems associated with making longitudinal comparisons based upon this normative information.

100

(2) *Examination of Test Data*—Rhode Island's State testing data for 1970-71 and 1974-75 analyzed public/parochial score differentials for the total score distributions. Prior State reports restricted the examination to simple average scores.

Data were obtained from information in the ITBS technical manuals provided by the Houghton-Mifflin Company; phone conversations with A. N. Hieronymus, the principal author of the ITBS; and the actual scores of all students who participated in the Rhode Island State testing program during the period 1969 to 1975.

Because of the focus of the study, it was deemed desirable to analyze the achievement scores of the same students at both the fourth and eighth grades. The most complete and reliable data set for this purpose was data on students who were fourth graders in 1970-71 and eighth graders in 1974-75.

School Setting Factors

Several differences were found between public and parochial schools during interviews: parochial school students missed fewer days of school per year (average 5.6) than public school students (average 9.1). Parochial school teachers were happier with the support and administrative activities in their buildings than public school teachers. In addition, parochial school teachers perceived disciplinary policy to be more effective in their schools than did public school teachers.

In relation to curriculum and instruction, several more differences were noted: parochial schools averaged more minutes of instruction in basic skills each week than public schools. In math instruction, parochial schools averaged 220 minutes per week while public schools averaged 193 minutes per week. In reading instruction, parochial schools average 620 minutes of instruction per week and public schools average 465.5 minutes per week.

Public schools engaged in a wider variety of academic activities (Table 1) (e.g., foreign language, science, math, and vocational courses) than parochial schools. Public schools also offered more "special" programs than parochial schools (e.g., special education, remedial math and reading, hearing classes, etc.).

In general, interview results indicated teachers perceive important differences between public and parochial students.

Public school teachers, particularly in low achieving schools, consistently rated their students as less eager to please, less motivated, less disciplined, less cheerful, less bright, and less interested in school. Parochial teachers rated their students as more cooperative, motivated, disciplined, cheerful, bright and high in school interest.

Table 1
PARTICIPATION IN SPECIAL PROGRAMS

Program Type	Achievement Level	School Type	Percents of Students Involved Grade 4	Grade 8
Bilingual	High	Public	2%	N.A.
		Parochial	N.A.*	N.A.
	Low	Public	4%	19%
		Parochial	N.A.	N.A.
Special Needs	High	Public	0%	1%
		Parochial	N.A.	N.A.
	Low	Public	4%	5%
		Parochial	N.A.	N.A.
Remedial Reading	High	Public	N.A.	31%
		Parochial	N.A.	N.A.
	Low	Public	11%	28%
		Parochial	47%	15%
Remedial Math	High	Public	8%	11%
		Parochial	N.A.	N.A.
	Low	Public	8%	16%
		Parochial	N.A.	29%
Other	High	Public	N.A.	19%
		Parochial	N.A.	N.A.
	Low	Public	7%	N.A.
		Parochial	N.A.	N.A.

* N.A. = Not applicable, indicating no program available in the schools interviewed.

In conclusion, the organizational environment of the parochial school in relation to discipline, teacher-principal relationship, and general climate was found to be more conducive to a positive learning environment.

In addition, the curriculum of the parochial school stressed the basic skills area while the public school curriculum was varied and dealt with more subject areas.

Population Factors

The examination of population factors focused on socio-economic status and achievement, i.e., examination of the background of students and its relationship to achievement; and on examination of specific demographic variables or selection factors which might affect average student achievement.

Data for examination of the population factors were collected from the interviews with teachers and administrators, responses to the short form questionnaire, and computer tape records of demographic information collected by the Rhode Island Department of Education during a statewide testing program.

With respect to population factors, a number of studies were found indicating that SES has been shown to be one of the most useful variables in predicting student achievement. Based upon this information, this research project attempted to ascertain if public school students and parochial school students differed in SES (Table 2).

In this regard, a higher percentage of parochial school students:

1. were female (fourth and eighth grades)
2. had books in their homes (fourth and eighth grades)
3. had books in their homes they liked to read (fourth and eighth grades)
4. owned library cards (fourth and eighth grades)
5. discussed school with their parents (eighth grades)
6. had parental assistance with school work (fourth grade)
7. had fathers whose occupation was clerical, professional, or managerial or owner (eighth grade)
8. had fathers who attended college (eighth grade)
9. desired to attend college (eighth grade)
10. preferred professional occupations (eighth grade).

On the basis of the data for both grades, it appears that a variety of demographic variables may at least contribute to the observed differences in parochial and public school achievement test results.

Information collected in the interviews suggests that no selection factors or entrance requirements to public or parochial schools are evidence other than religious affiliation.

103

Table 2

CORRELATIONS OF SELECTED DEMOGRAPHIC
SURVEY ITEMS WITH ITBS
COMPOSITE GRADE EQUIVALENT

	Grade 4		Grade 8	
	r*	p**	r*	p**
Item 5 (Number of People in House)	—.14	.001	—.09	.001
Item 7 (Number of Rooms in House)	.17	.001	.14	.001
Item 8 (Availability of Encyclopedia or Dictionary in House)	.22	.001	.10	.001
Item 9 (Availability of Newspapers or Magazines in the House)	.08	.001	.08	.001
Item 10 (Number of Books in the Home)	.26	.001	.26	.001
Item 11 (Student Interest in Books)	.10	.001	.14	.001
Item 12 (Student Possession of a Library Card)	.15	.001	.19	.001
Item 13 (Parent Communication about School)	.10	.001	.18	.001
Item 14 (Parent's Assistance with School Work)	—.09	.001	—.10	.001
Item 16 (Hours Spent Watching TV)	.08	.001	.02	.001
Item 21 (Student's Desire to go to College)	—.10	.001	.26	.001

* Pearson product-movement correlation
** Probability of achieving a r this large by chance

Selection factors or entrance requirements, as imposed by the public or parochial schools, are not variables which can explain differences in ITBS test results.

Interest in demographic data is due to the relationship of socioeconomic status to school achievement. All demographic variables in the State testing files for which it was suitable had correlations with ITBS composite grade equivalent score computed. Although many were statistically significant, all are indications of only slight relationships. In this data study, only the number of books in the home was substantially related to grade equivalent scores for both grades.

Psychometric and Test-Intrinsic Factors

In the examination of fourth to eighth grade achievement score changes it was noted that, for all ITBS subtests at both fourth and eighth grades, parochial school students scored higher than did public school students when both groups were compared to the national norms. This fact should not surprise anyone since, as is noted by the publishers of the ITBS, "In general, performance on the test by pupils in Catholic schools is extremely variable and is considerably above national performance, particularly in the upper grades." The important factor to consider is how to interpret these differences when inferences relative to the performance of the public and parochial schools is the issue. Examination of national and Catholic norms using the ITBS manuals indicates that grade equivalent scores associated with the various percentiles are substantially higher for the Catholic norm sample than for the national norm sample; there is typically a two to three month differential at fourth grade, and a four to eleven month differential at eighth grade. In examining the differences in achievement of the public and parochial school students on the Rhode Island State testing program, therefore, the following sets of analyses were conducted:

(a) examination of the test publishers' manuals based on national norms and norms for students in Catholic schools to determine what, if any, national patterns of achievement differences existed; and

(b) re-analysis of Rhode Island public and parochial school students' achievement compared with their most appropriate norm group or groups.

The results of these comparison are given in Tables 3 through 8. Table 3 presents, for each of four test areas, the average grade equivalents *and* the percentiles associated with these grade equivalents. Since a percentile represents standing within a specified population, the "expected change" from fourth to eighth grade would be 0—i.e., the expectation would be that the students would neither gain nor lose, but would maintain their relative position in the population. Inspection of Table 3 illustrates that, when change relative to the national norm group is examined, the average public school student decreased slightly (from a loss of between three to seven percentile points) while the average parochial school student increased slightly (from no change to a gain of two percentile points). Further, the average for the public school students started very close to the 50th percentile (the "national average") and ended very close to the national average. On the composite, or overall score, the change was from the 52nd to the 48th percentile. Parochial school students at the fourth grade level were somewhat above the national average (the 59th percentile) at grade four and improved very slightly (to the 60th percentile) by grade eight.

Table 3

ALTERNATIVE LONGITUDINAL COMPARISON (1970-71 TO 1974-75) OF THE LONGITUDINAL DATA PRESENTED BY GRADE

ITBS SCORE		4th Grade 1970-71		8th Grade 1974-75		Expected Gain	Actual Gain
		GE	Natl. %ile.	GE	Natl. %ile.	Natl. %ile.	Natl. %ile.
Composite	Public	4.1	52	7.9	48	0	—4
	Parochial	4.3	59	8.5	60	0	+1
Reading	Public	4.0	48	7.8	45	0	—3
	Parochial	4.3	56	8.5	57	0	+1
Total Language	Public	4.2	54	7.8	47	0	—7
	Parochial	4.6	63	8.8	63	0	0
Total Mathematics	Public	4.1	52	7.9	48	0	—4
	Parochial	4.1	52	8.2	54	0	+2

The data which follow are based on a re-analysis of student test scores from 1970-71 (fourth grade) and 1974-75 (eighth grade). It uses, as its measure of central tendency, the median score rather than the mean score, since: a) percentile scores represent an ordinal scale rather than an internal scale and thus are not proper to compute a mean; and b) the 50th percentile is, by definition, the median.

Examination of differences in student achievement are based on an examination of not only the differences between scores of the average (median) student, but also between students at other points in the distribution. Thus, the summarized findings which follow use two basic methods of analysis:

(1) statistical tests of significance for differences in cumu-
    lative frequency distributions at fourth and eighth
    grades based on national percentile norms and

(2) an examination of student scores at three critical points
    in the distribution: the 25th, 50th, and 75th percentiles
    based on Rhode Island scores.

Examination of the 25th, 50th, and 75th percentiles (Tables
4 and 5) of the fourth and eighth grade achievement scores for
public and parochial school students simply corroborated the
findings relative to the total score distribution—i.e., when national percentile norms are the common reference point for
gauging achievement score changes for public and parochial
schools, public schools demonstrate a slight "slippage" relative
to the national population, while parochial schools demonstrate
a slight increase in their standing relative to the national population. It should be noted that although the differences in total
score distributions were statistically significant, the actual net
amount of losses or gains was quite small.

Table 4

FOURTH TO EIGHTH GRADE ACHIEVEMENT CHANGES, PUBLIC SCHOOL STUDENT, COMPOSITE

| | Fourth Grade | | Eighth Grade | |
	G.E.	National Percentile	G.E.	National Percentile
P75	4.9	76	9.0	70
P50	4.2	56	7.8	46
P25	3.5	33	6.7	26

Table 5

FOURTH TO EIGHTH GRADE ACHIEVEMENT CHANGES, PAROCHIAL SCHOOL STUDENT, COMPOSITE

| | Fourth Grade | | Eighth Grade | |
	G.E.	National Percentile	G.E.	National Percentile
P75	4.9	76	10.0	77
P50	4.3	59	8.9	60
P25	3.7	40	7.5	40

Table 6 presents, for each of four ITBS test areas, the percentile ranks associated with the "average" public and parochial school student. For the public school students a single percentile

Table 6

ITBS ACHIEVEMENT OF FOURTH GRADERS BY TYPE OF SCHOOL (1970-71)

Percentile Rank

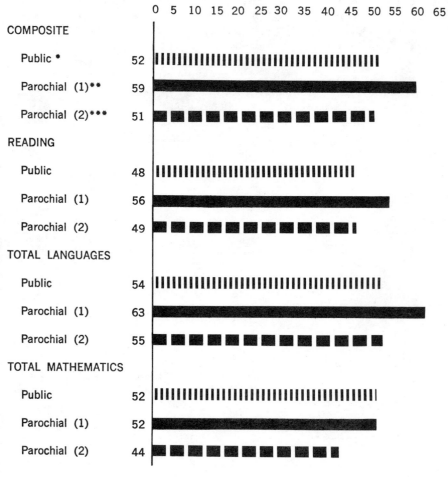

* Public: Using *National* Norms Tables
** Parochial (1): Using *National* Norms Tables
*** Parochial (2): Using *Catholic School* Norms Tables

rank, obtained from the national norms tables, is presented. For the parochial school fourth grades, however, *two* percentile ranks are presented—parochial (1), obtained from the national norms

Table 7

ITBS ACHIEVEMENT OF EIGHTH GRADERS BY TYPE OF SCHOOL
(1974-75)

Percentile Rank

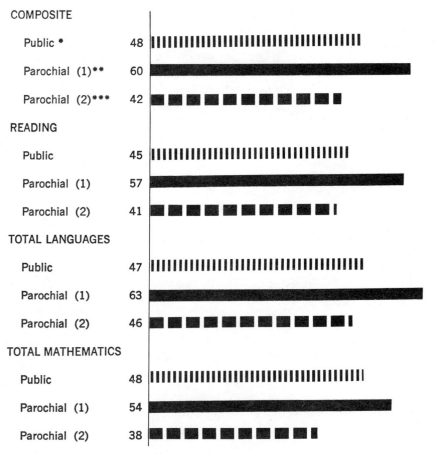

table and parochial (2), obtained from the norms table for Catholic schools. As inspection of Table 6 illustrates, the percentile for the average fourth grade public school student is below the percentile for the average fourth grade parochial student [parochial (1)] when both are compared to national norms. When the parochial school students are compared to what is perhaps a more appropriate reference group, the Catholic school norms, a somewhat different picture emerges. Comparing performance of public with parochial (2) indicates that when the public and parochial schools are compared to their most comparable reference group, their respective achievement relative to these groups is very close—on the ITBS Composite score the percentile ranks are 52 and 51 for the public and parochial schools, respectively.

Table 7 presents a similar picture at grade eight. As was the case at grade four, the absolute achievement level of the parochial school students exceeds that of the public school students when both are compared to the national norms [public vs. parochial (1)]. When comparisons are made vis-à-vis their more comparable reference group, however, a different picture emerges. While the public school students remain quite close to the center of their reference group (composite score percentile = 48) the parochial school students score moderately below the center of their (Catholic schools) reference group (composite score percentile rank = 42).

Finally, Table 8 displays achievement score changes from fourth to eighth grade for public and parochial school students, where changes are defined in terms of gains or losses in standing relative to one's norm group. As can be seen in Table 6, there are small to moderate decreases in Rhode Island public school students' standing relative to the national norms between fourth and eighth grades (losses range from three percentile points in reading to seven percentile points in total language). When Rhode Island parochial school student changes are examined relative to national norms [parochial (1)] it can be seen that these changes range from no change on the total language score to a gain of two percentile points on the total mathematics score. When Rhode Island parochial school student scores are compared to the norms for Catholic schools [parochial (2)] it can be seen that moderate decreases occur in percentile standing (losses range from six percentile points in total mathematics to nine percentile points on total language and the composite score).

Table 8

Fourth to Eighth Grade ITBS Achievement Changes by Type of School

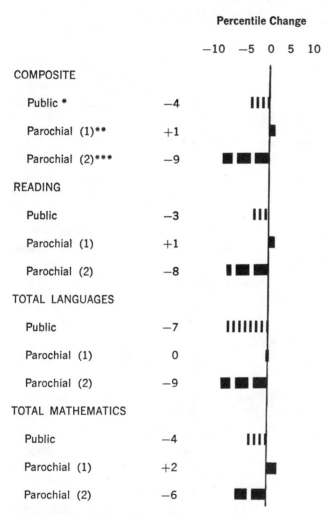

		Percentile Change
		−10 −5 0 5 10
COMPOSITE		
Public *	−4	
Parochial (1)**	+1	
Parochial (2)***	−9	
READING		
Public	−3	
Parochial (1)	+1	
Parochial (2)	−8	
TOTAL LANGUAGES		
Public	−7	
Parochial (1)	0	
Parochial (2)	−9	
TOTAL MATHEMATICS		
Public	−4	
Parochial (1)	+2	
Parochial (2)	−6	

* Public Using *National* Norms Tables
** Parochial (1): Using *National* Norms Tables
*** Parochial (2): Using *Catholic School* Norms Tables

SUMMARY

This investigation was undertaken to determine what factors might contribute to differences in student scores on the Iowa Test of Basic Skills between public and parochial schools. The design of the study was primarily that of descriptive data collection and reporting. The following differences were identified:

In the area of school setting factors:

    a. The amount of time spent in direct instruction of basic skills was greater in parochial schools where more time was spent teaching math and reading than public schools;

    b. Parochial schools have higher pupil/teacher ratios than public schools;

    c. The number of student absences for public school students was greater than for the parochial students;

    d. Parochial teachers felt discipline procedures in their school were more effective than did the public school teachers.

In the area of population factors:

    a. A difference in the percent of female students attending the parochial, as compared to the public, schools;

    b. Differing teacher perceptions of parental support in the public and in the parochial settings;

    c. Differing teacher perceptions of student motivational variables in the public and in the parochial settings; and

    d. Differences in the reported father's occupational status of parochial and public school students.

Finally, in the Psychometric/Test Intrinsic area:

    a. In relation to national norms, there are significant differences between the ITBS achievement test score distributions of public and parochial school students. These differences are larger at the eighth grade than at the fourth grade.

    b. In general, differences in ITBS score distributions based on national norms occur at the middle and lower end of the distribution. There are no substantial differences in achievement between public and parochial school students who score at the top of their respective distributions.

c. Differences in achievement between public and parochial school students are greatest in the subtest area of language and least in the subtest area of mathematics.